Dispatches
from the
Religious Left

The Future of Faith and Politics in America

Edited by Frederick Clarkson

Introduction by Joan Brown Campbell
Afterword by Jeff Sharlet

PUBLISHING

Brooklyn, New York

Printed in Michigan, U.S.A.
10 9 8 7 6 5 4 3 2 1

Please direct inquires to:

Ig Publishing
178 Clinton Avenue
Brooklyn, NY 11205

Library of Congress Cataloging-in-Publication Data

Dispatches from the religious left : the future of faith and politics in America
/
edited by Frederick Clarkson.
    p. cm.
 ISBN-13: 978-0-9788431-8-2
 ISBN-10: 0-9788431-8-5
 1. Religion and politics--United States. 2. United States--Religion. I.
Clarkson, Frederick.
 BL2525.D575 2009
 201'.720973--dc22

                                        2008032830

CONTENTS

PART II.
MEMOS ON HOT BUTTON ISSUES

PART III.
GETTING FROM HERE TO THERE

INTRODUCTION

⇦

REV. DR. JOAN BROWN CAMPBELL

"There is a time when silence is betrayal... that time is now."
—Abraham Heschel

Finally, the Religious Left has found its voice and is willing to own the prophetic tradition that has long characterized its sense of ministry. Religion that is biblically-based takes seriously the issues of poverty, prejudice, peace, and power. The health and well-being of God's children has always been the business of people of faith, and it has never been popular or universally well received.

Our respective religious traditions and the responsibilities and opportunities of constitutional democracy require us not to turn away from an engagement with the powers and principalities of our day. The question is not whether there should be interaction between faith and politics; rather the question is how progressive people of faith should engage in public life. The fact that the excesses of the Religious Right have in the eyes of many compromised the integrity of faith in public life should not deter progressive people from responsible citizenship.

The founders of this nation were in the main deeply religious people, and they were the revolutionaries of their day. The values imbedded in our historical documents are the values shared by every major faith...the inalienable rights of every person are to this day life, liberty, and the pursuit of happiness. And yet, in the name of religious liberty and the separation of church and state, good people of deep faith have come to believe that politics corrupts the purity of faith. This is a tragic misunderstanding of both faith and politics.

The writers in this challenging volume of essays reveal with clear focus how we might make more powerful strides toward justice, equality and peace without compromising our faith and without unjustly turning our government institutions into faith-based advocates for religious groups with a particular political bias. These writers remind us that faith has always challenged power on behalf of the lonely, the lost, and the forgotten. If this is Left, then let us claim it as an appropriate call to those whose lives are motivated by faith.

Editor Frederick Clarkson asked an eclectic group of writers, thinkers, and activists for their thoughts on what it would take to make a Religious Left that is greater than the sum of its current parts; a movement that could develop a greater capacity to achieve something that more closely resembles our highest aspirations for a just society. What could we be doing better, much better? In the face of looming global and local problems, essayist Daniel Schultz bluntly observes: "What the Religious Left is doing, isn't working." If we accept that premise, conscience requires that we reevaluate. This book does some of that, while not pretending that the job is anymore than just getting started. Such humility not withstanding, no one should be surprised to see some Conventional Wisdoms fundamentally questioned in this collection. But Clarkson says that this volume should not be taken as a platform, a manifesto, or a blueprint for the Religious Left. Instead, it is best read as a conversation starter, one intended to allow for a broadening and deepening of the kinds of discussions religious progressives need to be having.

This book is bursting with hope, and urgency and possibility from writers who are mostly not the "usual suspects," although in contributing to this book, they may have placed themselves in danger of being so defined. Nevertheless, they seem to have a clear sense of where they stand in history and in the great progressive traditions of which they are a part. Marshall Ganz, a veteran of the Civil Rights movement and the hey day of Cesar Chavez and United Farm Workers, who now teaches at Harvard, believes he now better understands what Hillel was talking about 2,000 years ago, while much younger leaders like Osagyefo Sekou and Kety Esquivel struggle with the contemporary meaning of Martin Luther King Jr.'s "Letter from Birmingham Jail."

This eclectic band of essayists are writing independently of one another and from different parts of the country, all coming out of different backgrounds and experiences. And they certainly show us many things we would not otherwise see or not otherwise notice, and leave us hungering for more. Undoubtedly, if we put them all in a room, they would not agree on all things. And that is as it should be. But I think it would be fair to say that a rough consensus exists for this much: Standing for clear principles while remaining attentive to, but unswayed by, political fashions; understanding our respective faith traditions in the context of the history of our constitutional democracy; respecting the right of religious difference and separation of church and state; and always reevaluating our tactics, strategy and resources in light of our experience; and acting on what we have learned. If this is so, that sounds like a Religious Left that is faithful to its highest calling.

Let the conversation begin!

Joan Brown Campbell
Chautauqua Institution
August 13, 2008

Editor's Introduction: A Religious Left for the 21st Century?

⇐

FREDERICK CLARKSON

When Ig Publishing asked me if I'd consider putting together what became this anthology, I was skeptical at first. My experience and expertise over the years has mostly been writing about the Religious Right—therefore I wasn't sure that I was the right person for the job. But then I reminded myself that my roots are in progressive religious politics that go back to the 1970s when, after college, I served on the staff of Clergy and Laity Concerned (CALC). CALC was an interfaith outgrowth of Clergy and Layman Concerned about Vietnam, founded by Reverend William Sloan Coffin, Rabbi Abraham Heschel and Dr. Martin Luther King Jr., in opposition to the war in Vietnam. CALC had updated and built on the religious anti-war experience with a broader agenda and a more inclusive organizational name. I eventually moved on, as did CALC.

Since then, I have worked closely with progressive religious leaders and organizations on a variety of projects. And while my knowledge of the progressive religious political landscape needed updating, I felt that my knowledge of the history and political dynamics of the Religious Right was a particular strength to draw on as we contemplated a Religious Left for the twenty-first century. In short, I changed my mind. I can say now with great assurance that knowledge of the differences and the different histories of the Religious Right and the Religious Left is not merely a happy extra, but I would argue, is a necessary prerequisite for envisioning what a more politically dynamic Religious Left could be in twenty-first century America. Sorting out the differences, and discussing what we can learn from formidable opponents, as well as what we must not emulate, is one of the themes of this book.

Indeed, to paraphrase Mark Twain, reports of the death of the Religious Right have been "greatly exaggerated." In truth, the movement is neither dead nor dying, as pundits periodically declare, but is in a state of transition, particularly as the founding generation of leaders passes from the scene. But whatever its ups and downs, it remains one of the most significant social and political movements in modern American history—and there is nothing on the left that is even remotely comparable.

So before I say a few words about *Dispatches from the Religious Left*, here are a few thoughts about the Religious Right. The Religious Right is a movement that has been best known by a number of major politically oriented ministries and major political organizations operating primarily (but not exclusively) within the Republican Party. However, there is much more to it, as the movement has institutionalized on a scale that is not widely appreciated. A growing number of think tanks, political and media entities, publishing houses, colleges, universities and even law schools affiliated with the Religious Right already play a significant role in American public life, and this is unlikely to change much, even with the recent rise in the fortunes of the Democratic Party and the passing of the leaders of the founding generation of the Religious Right. Indeed, the movement's institutional infrastructure; the ideologies they have promoted; the books they have written; the generations of political activists they have trained and deployed; and the politicians they have elected to office at all levels, and those who aspire to office will be with us for a long time to come.

Meanwhile, the contemporary Religious Left is sufficiently diffuse that it does not really even qualify as a movement in the broad, social science sense of the term. However, as Daniel Schultz puts it in his essay, "What the Religious Left is doing isn't working," this observation is not intended as an insult, but rather as a blunt assessment of the current state of the "movement." This observation is not intended as an insult, but rather as a blunt assessment of the current state of the "movement." There are many good people involved in progressive religion who are doing great things, and many excellent organizations making strides against the odds. But as any good political organizer, any good businessperson, any good baseball coach—in short, any good leader—will tell you that you have to reevaluate when things are not going well. While religious progressives are concerned about a host of matters—preventing and stopping wars, alleviating poverty, saving the environment, righting racial injustices—much of what is being done is not working, or not working well enough. And, even considering those things that are working well, how can the Religious Left become greater than the sum of its parts? This book is about launching a wide ranging conversation of reevaluation in order to discover what it would take for the Religious Left to become more politically effective.

Unfortunately, our country's experience of the Religious Right has left a bad taste in the mouths of many, leading some to recoil at the very idea of a Religious Left. This is an understandable reaction—but only up to a point. A prospective Religious Left would be in no way analogous to the Religious Right, and to suggest anything otherwise is an exercise in false equivalence. A Religious Left deserves to be heard and evaluated on its own terms. If this volume is any indication, whatever an authentic, revitalized Religious Left turns out to be, it will not be a fun house mirror image of the worst elements of the Religious Right. "Progressive religious groups," Peter Laarman observes in his essay, "have a deep understanding of the need for separation of church and state woven into their DNA." A Religious Left conceived in this way, would be of a profoundly different nature than the Religious Right. And that is just for starters.

That said, *Dispatches* is not a manifesto, a platform or a blueprint for the Religious Left. And participation in *Dispatches* does not necessarily imply agreement among the writers. Rather, this is a collection of bold, energetic, highly responsible and forward-looking essays that ask good questions; tell good stories; locate us in history and in our political moment; call for a vision of a brighter future, as well as offering some serious ideas about what needs to be done, and done differently. Part of what these essays do is to model ways of thinking from a variety of perspectives: clergy and laity; activists and academics; journalists; think tankers; professional issue advocates, and various combinations thereof. These are some of the kinds of people that comprise a movement, and no one sector dominates this volume.

But there is one feature I want to highlight. Herein are some remarkable examples of how progressive religious people think and write when unencumbered by the dictates of contemporary fashions in "faith outreach" by candidates for major offices; or framed solely by areas of "common ground" with conservative evangelicals and conservative Catholics. Such activities may be fine, but they do not define what a Religious Left is or should be. Religious progressives cannot, and should not be expected to, elide their deeply held values or be asked to sacrifice the human and civil rights of whole classes of people in the interest of short term political expediency. Astute progressives understand the art of politics includes dialog and compromise, but dialog and compromise are not to be conflated with capitulation, self-marginalization, and betrayal.

A serious discussion of a movement that arises from the values and visions of the great religious social justice traditions will undoubtedly discomfit some—maybe most of us. Nevertheless, I hope that *Dispatches from the Religious Left* will encourage and inform the kinds of meaningful, spirited and constructive conversations from which people come away transformed, recognizing that new directions are not only necessary, but possible.

PART I.

Envisioning A More Politically Dynamic Religious Left

HILLEL'S QUESTIONS:
A CALL FOR LEADERSHIP

⇐

Dr. Marshall Ganz

If I am not for myself, who will be for me? When I am for myself alone, what am I? If not now, when?

What can our struggle to answer Hillel's questions teach us about congregational leadership, community, and work in the world?

I began my journey as the son of a rabbi and teacher in Bakersfield, California, found myself called to public work in the civil rights movement in Mississippi, discovered a vocation for organizing, and, in the fall of 1965, joined Cesar Chavez in his efforts to unionize farm workers. After twenty-eight years "in the field," I returned to Harvard, where I now teach a rising generation of students how to turn our shared values into the power to repair ourselves, our community, and our world. This is the work of organizing.

Only as I began to do the work did I learn how central this calling is to our tradition. It may have begun with Moses—an insider outsider, a Jew who was an Egyptian, a man of the oppressed, raised in the house of the oppressor, a man who knew the world's pain but who, at God's insistence, found he could lead others on a journey of redemption. And only as I began to look for words to teach this craft—developing leadership, building community, and taking public action — did I really hear the questions Hillel asked 2000 years ago.

If I am not for myself, who will be for me? We are created in God's image—each of infinite moral worth, capable of choice, and utterly unique—but our days are finite, our reach is limited, and we have more to learn than we can ever know. We begin as the children of our parents. As we embrace them and struggle with them, we begin authoring who we are in relation to them. As "works in progress," we grow as siblings, friends, lovers, students, workers, colleagues, congregants, and citizens. Many of us become parents ourselves. In facing challenges, making choices, and living with consequences, in both sorrow and joy, we learn to love what we love, know what we know, and do what we do. To be "for myself" is to honor the sources of my worth, my strengths, and my limitations.

To find the courage, commitment, and hopefulness to face the challenges of our times, why would we turn to marketing mavens, management gurus, and niche strategists when our real sources of strength are in learning who we are, where we come from, and where we are going?

When I am for myself alone, what am I? The implication is powerful. When I think only of myself, I lose my humanity. No longer a "who," I have become a "what." To be a "self" is to be in relationship with "others" and with God. It is not an option, but is woven into the very fabric of our lives.

Who can better understand this than a people whose collective "self," whose identity, is formed in covenant, whose worship is in community, and whose relationship with God is intertwined in relationship with one another?

To be in relationship is about justice, not charity. Relationship requires recognition of the "other" as a "self" equally created in God's image, unique, and capable of choice. It is to do "with" the other, not "to" the other. Entering into "relationship with" requires speaking and listening; exploring values, interests, and resources; discerning commonalities and differences; committing to a shared project. Understood in this way, relationship is demanding because it requires giving of ourselves, not only of our goods. But this is also why it is so powerful.

To find sources of renewal, we begin by revitalizing old relationships and creating new ones, through which we can question what we have not before questioned, learn what we have not yet learned, identify common purposes, turn differences into collaboration, and create shared capacity.

Although we begin within our congregations, this is only a beginning. Doesn't Hillel want us to understand that only by reaching out to others can we fully realize the capacity that lies within ourselves? This is as true for congregations, communities, and nations as it is for individuals. Our instruction to be a "blessing to the nations" does not mean "giving charity to"; it means "entering into relationship with."

If not now, when? Does this mean that the only things worth doing are what we can do right now? Hillel's question implies that unless reflection and relationship result in action — in world-changing work—it is self-indulgence. Action requires the commitment of time, money, and energy. Committing resources requires making choices. And making choices shapes who we are. By taking action we not only change the world around us, we also change ourselves. But creative action is challenging—risky, uncertain, and ambiguous. We can never learn to do it if we remain in the Garden, where all is given to us. Because it is challenging, we are easily caught in what Tolstoy called "the snare of preparation"— a little more study, a little more planning, a little more certainty. So Hillel's question teaches us that changing ourselves and our world depends on creative action, the capacity that flows not from our status as "knowers," experts who have all the answers, but from our courage as "learners"—questioners with the faith that we can learn to create a new world only by creating it.

To find the strength to renew ourselves—as individuals, congregations, or communities—where do we turn? Hillel guides us to the insight that the challenges of leadership, community, and work in the world—particularly the work of justice—do not each stand on their own, but are linked to each other. And our power to do the work of justice grows out of the relationships we build with one another. The motivation to build relationships with one another grows out of the recognition that we can only become complete selves by doing so. It is not complicated—just difficult. We must commit our time, imagination, and hearts. We must engage with each other in newly challenging ways. And we must find the courage to risk creative action. The job of leadership is to make this happen; this craft—rooted in the work of Moses—is what organizing is all about.

Reprinted with permission from Sh'ma: A Journal of Jewish Responsibility (www.shma.com) January 2007

THE RELIGIOUS LEFT: CHANGING THE SCRIPT

⇐

REV. DANIEL SCHULTZ

When Fred Clarkson asked me to contribute an essay to this collection, I immediately set about detailing the demographic, organizational, philosophical and theological differences between the Religious Right and the Religious Left. I plotted out a detailed examination of these qualities, using public opinion surveys, voting data, organizational charts and religious history.

Two and a quarter pages and nine footnotes into the project, I was hopelessly bogged down.

For the record, I still believe there is value in a thorough sociological examination of the Religious Left and what makes it unique. Mercifully, what needs to be said for the present purposes is simple:

What the Religious Left is doing is not working!

We on the Religious Left are bedeviled by a number of problems, if you'll excuse the phrase. What follows are several points of bedevilment—and some thoughts about the way out of this bedevilment.

First of all, we are far too varied and complex a movement

to speak with one voice. We are made up of congregations, denominational offices from local to national levels, other religious representatives, ecumenical and interfaith organizations, social-justice and peace activists, single-issue groups, Washington insiders, Democratic Party outreach initiatives, seminaries, institutes, and bloggers. None of us work the same way, or on precisely the same concerns. And where secular progressives have to deal with political and strategic differences, religious liberals also have to factor in theological and ecclesiastical gaps. In many ways, our diversity is our core strength, but this diversity also requires a common, coherent, strategic vision. Currently, we do not have one.

While things have started to get better since Faith in Public Life, an outgrowth of the Center for American Progress, arrived on the scene following the 2004 elections, a persistent lack of organization and funding for infrastructure across the movement has caused our messaging to be diffused and ineffective. This leads to the perception that we don't believe in much of anything. It also doesn't help that for a movement based on religious values, we have an odd tendency to lose ourselves in the fog of *issues*.

One classic example of this tendency was a press release issued by the National Council of Churches the day before the 2004 election to call on the Bush administration to repatriate Uighur prisoners held at Guantanamo Bay. The reaction of Amy Sullivan in an article for the *Washington Monthly* the following March was caustic, but on-target: "I have no doubt that advocacy on behalf of Chinese Muslim prisoners is a worthy cause," she wrote. "I also have no doubt that it confirms the irrelevance of the once-powerful religious left."[1] Much of the malfeasance of the Bush administration was well known before the 2004 election. A relevant religious voice would have asked about the rush to war, Abu Ghraib, or the inexcusable immorality of the Guantanamo prison itself. The NCC chose instead to target a single, narrowly-defined issue. By not "breaking the frame" of the debate, the Religious Left has often conceded morally unacceptable situations before the fight has even begun.

The Religious Left is also split between spiritual development and political action. Progressive religion has long been uncomfortable with conflating the two, unlike our conservative counterparts. This tension, coupled with long-term membership declines, has led some Protestant denominations to withdraw from the public square. Religious front groups for right-wing political and financial interests such as the Institute on Religion and Democracy have happily encouraged this trend with well-funded campaigns to paint the churches' leadership as radical leftists, and by stoking internal denominational disputes. Despite the meddling, some denominations have embraced a liberal political or public policy identity. But the reality is that for many reasons—cultural, numerical, and theological— the Protestant mainline and the "social Catholics" are no longer as visible as they once were.

Let's not let ourselves off the hook, either. For many faithful progressives, ambivalence is the emotion of first resort when considering politics. Because we tend to define faith over and against the dirty, judgmental business of winning elections, we are, unsurprisingly, reluctant to jump into the partisan shark tank. Therefore, some of us pursue "spiritual activism," or understand "progressive" to modify theology more than politics. Others have become embittered commentators on the state of a game they refuse to play. And many maintain an uneasy line between religious and political commitments without ever being able to give their hearts undivided to either side. This conflict is particularly acute for Christians raised on sermons about loving one's enemy or being "in the world, but not of it."

In many ways, all of this creates a healthy, even fruitful tension. And, as we shall see, one of the unique strengths our movement can leverage is our moral authority. That authority is only increased by the ability to stay out of petty political bickering. But it is equally true that the Religious Left's claim to influence on public affairs has been withered by its general failure to address the aggression of movement conservatism. (Some right-wing evangelicals don't even consider progressive believers to be Christians.) No doubt this is largely influenced by the perception that we won't stand to testify for our beliefs. What's more, many progressive activists without deep ties to religious communities are confused by the Religious Left's apparent powerlessness and silence before the reactionary elements of Christianity, and harshly critical of its refusal to articulate a simple, clear and effective moral critique of conservative ideas and policies. However Christ-like we may be in our ethical approaches, as a political movement we are in danger of being declared neither hot nor warm—and being spit out accordingly.

A PRESCRIPTION FOR THE RELIGIOUS LEFT: POLITICAL THEOLOGY

So much for the diagnosis. Now, what is to be done? First off, we know what doesn't work, as ignoring the political dimension of faith in favor of spirituality without context has lost mainline churches a generation of believers. For belief to be relevant, it must demonstrate that it makes a difference in this world *and* the next.

Whining that progressives have values, too, accomplishes nothing. Instead, it keeps alive conservative frames about "amoral liberals" without offering a meaningful alternative. In addition, trying to make the Democratic Party more "friendly to faith" in order to draw "persuadable" social conservatives is, frankly, a waste of resources. This is likely to be a controversial assertion, as many progressives want to establish as broad a coalition as possible, and see nothing wrong with being "faith friendly." Unfortunately, this strategy does not provide a positive vision, but only offers a defensive reaction to conservative criticism. Even if, as seems possible, we are entering an era of Democratic dominance of national politics and government, there is no need to water down the identity of a nascent Religious Left by soft-pedaling core social beliefs in order to reach swing voters.

Similarly, the idea that the Religious Left can somehow show the nation a kinder, gentler way to do politics without partisanship is also useless. On a practical level, voters have demonstrated again and again that they want Democrats to provide a meaningful alternative to the reactionary ideology of the Republican Party. The progressive agenda is a popular one, while conservatism represents an ever-smaller slice of the electorate. Again, there is no political need to compromise with a radical movement that is declining in popularity.

Ethically, this seemingly principled desire to accomplish something "beyond politics" while remaining engaged with the political system rests on dubious assertions. It assumes that there is some divine shortcut to solving political problems that somehow does not involve politics. In truth, there is no such transcendent way. Until the Kingdom come, those who want to create and sustain social change are stuck with morally ambiguous involvement in the world of partisan politics. Those who want to keep their hands clean should find another hobby or withdraw from the political realm altogether. Pacifists like Stanley Hauerwas will be happy to point the way.

The eagerness to heal politics also involves the perverse notion that one party should be allowed to drag the nation through an almost infinite variety of dirty tricks, at the end of which the other party should let bygones be bygones. However satisfactory that might be to those raised on an ethos of turning the other cheek, it does little to establish justice. Many wrongs have been committed during the conservative ascendancy of the past forty years. They will need to be set right. This is not a time to cry "peace, peace" when in fact there is no peace. This is a time to articulate a *political theology*. By this I mean a normative politics rooted in "a view of God and his purposes, and their relation to human action in history, even though our normative thought doesn't derive directly from any theological premises, revealed or rationally arrived at," to borrow a quick-and-dirty definition from the philosopher and social critic Charles Taylor.

The Religious Left needs to put forward a simple, clear and effective moral critique not just of conservatism, but of all American life. This critique must lay out clear ethical distinctions, and suggest the political (but not necessarily partisan) choices that have be made as a result.

But a workable progressive political theology should be consistent with broadly progressive values, yet incisive enough that it is able to establish clear responsibility for living up to those values. It must offer insight into social, cultural, economic and political problems. It is not enough to say, for example, that "fighting poverty is a moral value." Voters must understand not only what the value is, but why it is important and who they should hold accountable if it is not upheld. In short, a workable progressive ideology must create a standard for judging the contemporary political scene.

THE POLITICAL THEOLOGY OF WALTER BRUEGGEMANN

In a 2005 *Christian Century* article, the Old Testament scholar and theologian Walter Brueggemann laid out nineteen theses about the Bible's counter-cultural witness to our society. Brueggemann discerned the presence of "scripts" in our lives: dynamic, normative stories that actualize our values in patterns of behavior, often below the threshold of consciousness. The Biblical narrative of relationship with what Brueggemann terms the "elusive, irascible God" calls these scripts into question. The God of Abraham, Isaac and Ishmael is a jealous God, and will brook no divided loyalties.

The primary script in control of our lives, according to Brueggemann, "the script of therapeutic, technological, consumer-

ist militarism that permeates every dimension of our common life."
By this, he means certain acculturated assumptions about the way
life should work. Brueggemann writes:

> • "I use the term therapeutic to refer to the assumption
> that there is a product or a treatment or a process to coun-
> teract every ache and pain and discomfort and trouble, so
> that life may be lived without inconvenience.

> • I use the term technological, following Jacques Ellul, to
> refer to the assumption that everything can be fixed and
> made right through human ingenuity; there is no issue so
> complex or so remote that it cannot be solved.

> • I say consumerist, because we live in a culture that believes
> that the whole world and all its resources are available to us
> without regard to the neighbor, that assumes more is bet-
> ter and that 'if you want it, you need it.' Thus there is now
> an advertisement that says: "It is not something you don't
> need; it is just that you haven't thought of it."

> • The militarism that pervades our society exists to protect
> and maintain the system and to deliver and guarantee all
> that is needed for therapeutic technological consumerism.
> This militarism occupies much of the church, much of the
> national budget and much of the research program of uni-
> versities."[2]

This script, says Brueggemann, promises to make us "safe and happy,"
yet has been a miserable failure. For our health and the health of the
world, we must let it go and grasp a new one. Though his aim is to
strengthen the theology of the church, not assist in partisan ideology,
Brueggemann describes this in straightforwardly political terms:

It is clear to all but the right-wing radio talk people and the sponsoring neoconservatives that the reach of the American military in global ambition has served only to destabilize and to produce new and deep threats to our society. The charade of a national security state has left us completely vulnerable to the whim of the very enemies that our security posture has itself evoked. A by-product of such attempts at security, moreover, has served in astonishing ways to evoke acrimony in the body politic that makes our democratic decision making processes nearly unworkable. We are not safe, and we are not happy. The script is guaranteed to produce new depths of insecurity and new waves of unhappiness. And in response to new depths of insecurity and new waves of unhappiness, a greater resolve arises to close the deal according to the script, which produces ever new waves and new depths.

This is a more insightful analysis of the current state of the union than anything I've ever read in corporate journalism. Brueggemann has sussed-out the framework that underlies much of our contemporary politics, and the utter faithlessness of its premises.

Which is not to say that this is a perfect vision. I would add one piece: we live in a *conformist* culture that relieves the anxiety of difference by attempting to synthesize, domesticate or co-opt all that cannot be easily digested. This is most readily seen in the tensions that swirl around cultural, racial and sexual diversity, but it is also reflected in the unhealthy desire of many pundits and politicians to establish "bipartisanship" without confronting real difference. However, bland unity and cheap healing are not progressive religious values. The God of the Old and New Testaments is often radically, even inexplicably "Other" from humanity. God's sovereign work of reconciliation should never be mistaken for "reaching across the aisle to get things done."With this addition, we have the ingredients of a workable political theology.

Brueggemann's critique couldn't be simpler or more clear. Though it is not shy about evaluating moral or political stances, its targets go well beyond a single ideology to attack shared, flawed assumptions. Attempting to live life without contingency or responsibility to others is wrong and unsustainable. That, it seems to me, is the central critique progressive faith can offer, and we ought to jump on it with both feet.

Putting Counterscripts Into Play

New York Democratic state senator Eric Schneiderman recently described the difference between what he calls *transactional* and *transformational* politics. The first is the simple and pragmatic art of securing the best possible deal given today's circumstances, while the second is "the work we do today to ensure that the deal we can get on gun control or immigration reform in a year—or five years, or 20 years—will be better than the deal we can get today." Schneiderman's description of this process makes it seem tailor-made for the Religious Left:

> "Transformational politics requires us to challenge the way people think about issues, opening their minds to better possibilities. It requires us to root out the assumptions about politics or economics or human nature that prevent us from embracing policies that will make our lives better."[3]

Questioning assumptions, imagining new possibilities, keeping an eye on the human bottom line of public policy: this is the natural work of faithful people engaged in an ongoing ethical encounter with a dynamic God. God is still speaking indeed, still working to re-create our world, and we should be fearless in proclaiming the social and political implications of that reality.

If we can do so, we will take control of the so-called Overton Window, the spectrum of "commonly held ideas, attitudes and presumptions [that] frame what is politically possible."[4] By using the moral authority traditionally accorded to religious leaders in America, we can influence which ideas are or are not considered acceptable in political discourse.

This work is taking place already, as various formations of the media seek to balance the domineering voice of the Religious Right with voices from the "new" Religious Left. However, we need to push the media beyond "usual suspects" like Tony Campolo, Michael Lerner, or Jim Wallis. But that's relatively easily done, especially in a time when media opportunities for the Religious Left seem to be growing. If we can come together around counterscripts, it will allow us to work across both partisan and confessional lines, an area of major concern for our new movement. This will enable us to critique both Democrats and Republicans, and perhaps even to establish new coalitions based on shared values. And because it relies on shared observation rather than revelation or a single theological framework, it will allow us to hold together both secular and religious progressives.

Brueggemann's Biblical theses are faithful—and progressive. They do not sell out or tone down for political convenience the kind of values articulated by George Lakoff's Rockridge Institute: strength, safety and protection, fulfillment, fairness, freedom, opportunity, prosperity, community, cooperation, trust, honesty, and openness. But they do ask in a distinctly religious voice to what end we uphold those values and whether they are ultimate or partial goals?

Establishing accountability through counterscripts is fairly simple. No politician will ever be able to usher in the Kingdom of God, of course, even if they were able to move the nation as a whole away from destructive scripts to healthier ways of being. But as a relative matter, evaluating the extent of their cooperation with the technological, therapeutic, consumerist, conformist or militarist scripts is almost as simple as opening the *Congressional Record*.[5]

In order to do this, we will have to lose our scruple about calling things for what they are. Prophets who are unwilling to judge present realities against a vision of God's possibilities are by definition unnecessary. Standing in judgment, however, goes against the grain of many religious progressives. Developing a righteous anger may therefore be the most difficult change to make— but also the most necessary.

COUNTERSCRIPTS: JUDGMENT, AMBIGUITY AND NEW GROUND

We are not safe, and we are not happy. This frank evaluation is the starting point for any meaningful conversation about the current state of our nation. If we on the Religious Left want to find relevance beyond easy slogans and "me-too-ism," then we will have to find a way to help our fellow citizens understand how to reorder their commitments in light of the scripts' failure to perform as advertised. Otherwise, the Religious Left will be remaindered as a not-particularly-effective electoral adjunct to the centrist wing of the Democratic Party.

How might we start this conversation in a way that advances the progressive cause yet honors "a view of God and his purposes"? That, of course, is the question of questions. And we will hear many answers to it in the years to come. Brueggemann for his part is explicit that his statements are theology, not utilitarian politics:

> "Liberals tend to get so engaged in the issues of the day, urgent and important as those issues are, that we forget that behind such issues is a meta-narrative that is not about our

particular social passion but about the world beyond our control. The claim of that alternative script is that there is at work among us a Truth that makes us safe, that makes us free, that makes us joyous in a way that the comfort and ease of the consumer economy cannot even imagine."

For a number of reasons, it will not be easy for religious progressives to work toward the counterscripting of our present society. Scripture guides us to build an alternative society in the countercultural world of the church, not to attempt the redemption of the public square. Moreover, the God Brueggemann has in sight is not an easy boss, nor is the textual container for his good news always user-friendly. Though the tensions between secular and religious liberals are often overstated, they do exist, and they will continue for the simple reason that their experiences and overarching goals, though they overlap, are not identical.

Perhaps most vexing of all, the judgment of the God Walter Brueggemann knows often drags us before our own ambivalence and forces us to face it:

> "One of the crucial tasks of ministry is to name the deep ambiguity that besets us, and to create a venue for waiting for God's newness among us. This work is not to put people in crisis. The work is to name the crisis that people are already in, the crisis that evokes resistance and hostility when it is brought to the surface and named.
>
> • God may yet lead us anew where liberals and conservatives can disrupt the shrillness long enough to admit that variously we are frightened by alternative patterns of sexuality. We do not want to kill all gays as the book of Leviticus teaches, but we are in fact uneasy about changes that seem so large.

• God may yet lead us anew when conservatives and liberals can interrupt our passion for consumer goods and lower taxes long enough to admit that we believe neighbors should be cared for, even with taxes. We have a passion for social programs but are nonetheless aware of being taxed excessively, and it causes us alarm.

• God may yet lead us so that liberals and conservatives can stop the loudness to know that the divestment that costs us nothing is too easy, whether directed at Israel or the Palestinians; the core divestment to which we are first called comes closer to our own entitlements. The Spirit has always been, for the church and beyond the church, 'a way out of no way.'"

This will no doubt make many progressives squirm. There are good reasons for that. Brueggemann addresses here the work of the church, not the state or society, and the work of the church is to stay together above all else. In that it is no less political than any other venue of human activity, but it is a politics directed at a certain aim—unity—that does not always map well onto larger spheres.

Then there is the less than full-throated support for a progressive agenda, particularly on questions of sexual identity, a difficulty Brueggemann himself points out. But the essential insight seems correct: there are any number of issues where honesty compels us to admit to conflicted feelings. More importantly, there are any number of issues where honesty compels us to challenge our self-perception as morally pure agents. It is precisely at such junctures where we might look for fertile new ground, spiritually and politically.

Take one of Brueggemann's examples quoted above. We might say that 9/11 has left our society ambivalent about what it means to be safe in an age of terror. Such a statement does not require us to surrender the belief that the Bush administration has seriously undermined democratic liberty and the rule of law in its zeal to erect an American security state. It has. Nor must we give up the argument that a reckless administration compromised national security in a rush to conduct an ill-considered, risky, and unnecessary war. It did. But we should also confess that many of us enabled this administration's lunacy by "supporting the troops" if not actually voting for Bush and Cheney. Certainly, we have all paid for the administration's malfeasance with our tax dollars, and benefited from the militarism it exploits.

Once we have admitted our moral compromises before and after September 2001, we can begin to recognize an opportunity for transformation. The attacks on New York, Pennsylvania and Washington D.C. should have sparked a reconsideration of an already dangerously unbalanced American security policy. That rethinking is now long overdue. Until we are able to surface and address our ambiguous desires to be kept safe and free, that rethinking will remain undone, and we will continue to be subject to "the charade of a national security state" in one form or another because we will not have changed the crucial assumption that the force of arms alone can keep us safe. That keeps us wedded to the morality of violence and the politics of militarism.

Working with such deeply embedded scripts may blunt the transactional effectiveness of the Religious Left in the short run. We can seldom offer a promised land, as it were, only an ongoing journey with a cranky, temperamental God and a destination that is perpetually just around the corner. There is a reason Brueggemann speaks of where "God may yet lead us." An honest faith demands that we admit that we have no idea where exactly God is directing us. After all, we've never been "there" before.

Again, this will be distressing for those who look to progressive faith to provide an electoral counterweight to the right-wing idolatry of power. They no doubt will want to know what religious believers can contribute toward securing the immediate electoral or governmental fortunes of a resurgent progressive movement. And there is no reason they shouldn't. Politics as it is currently designed is a short-range, bottom-line oriented business. If you can't deliver money or votes, then you have no power. The Religious Right is able to bring both to the table; therefore they still have considerable power.

But I hope that what I have been able to demonstrate in this analysis is that transactional politics is not our calling. *What the Religious Left has been doing does not work because we are meant to ask the questions, not line up behind the answers.* Where the Religious Right has been the cash machine and ground troops for the conservative movement, the Religious Left can and should be the engine for transformational progressive politics. And where religious conservatives have been the stout defenders of everything that is clear and solid and unchanging, religious progressives are the "astronauts of inner space," relentlessly pushing through uncertainty toward newer, higher ground. We ought to take it as a good sign when that drive "evokes resistance and hostility" and charges of judgmentalism. It means we're making progress.

The genius of the Religious Left has never been in organizational heft or the ability to mobilize campaign contributions or stick to talking points pumped out of the blast-faxes of suburban Virginia. Progressive faith has been generative instead in its eternal, persistent, damnably disruptive questioning of the seemingly self-evident way things must be. We are meant to be gadflies in the service of Lord, asking through political theologies difficult questions about what truly makes us safe, what truly makes us happy, and what truly brings us together across the divisions imposed by our society.

That last question is worth reflecting on another time. For now it is enough to recall the old joke that says the purpose of good preaching ought to be to comfort the afflicted and afflict the comfortable. I think that applies in spades to the Religious Left. There is and always has been a temptation to define religious progressives by the issues or the parties they have backed. It is a temptation that should be resisted. We are, and always have been, a ragged, disputatious lot following a ragged, disputatious narrative toward an irascible, hidden God. What has worked for us hasn't been a comfortable groove, but affliction and an inborn, restless stubbornness that forever keeps us asking questions instead of supplying the answers. That is hardly less complex than the "demographic, organizational, philosophical and theological differences" I set out to detail, and there are times when it seems hardly less satanic. But it is the faith we know, and most days, with God's help, it suffices. I'd suggest that any group that purports to call itself the Religious Left start there and work its way forward, slowly, tentatively, and with one eye always set firmly on where God may yet lead us.

NOTES

1. Amy Sullivan, "The Good Fight," *Washington Monthly,* March 2005, http://www.washingtonmonthly.com/features/2005/0503.sullivan. html

2. All Brueggemann quotes are from "Counterscript: living with the elusive God," published in *Christian Century* November 29, 2005 and adapted from an earlier speech.

3. "Transforming the Liberal Checklist," *Nation,* March 10, 2008. Hat tip, as always, to Digby.

4. Nathan J. Russell, "An Introduction To the Overton Window of Political Possibilities," Mackinac Center For Public Policy, http://www.mackinac.org/article.aspx?ID=7504

5. To forestall the inevitable snickers, let me stipulate that there will always be ways for crafty pols to hide their records in the complexity of governance in a nation of 300 million people. Which means that there will always be a need for sharp-eyed critics tuned to the artful dodge.

Not By Outrage Alone

REV. DR. KATHERINE HANCOCK RAGSDALE

I want to live in a world that values cooperation over competition; compassion over punishment; respect over control; and the dazzling diversity of creation over conformity. I dream of a world where every human being is cherished, in her and for her own particularity, and is, therefore, assured of food, education, health care, and meaningful work; where hospitality and mutual concern are the norm—in our homes, at our borders, and across this ever-shrinking globe. I long for a world where we fight with one another passionately about how best to achieve justice and freedom and peace, but such fights are grounded in mutual respect and a firm commitment to honesty and "seeking the truth come whence it may cost what it will." (Phillips Brooks, 1835-1893) And I want to know, I need to know, *your vision.* What do you see that this White, Southern (US), lesbian, feminist, activist Episcopal priest cannot see from where I stand or because other things have captured my attention? I want to spend my life fighting for something bigger than the reach of my own sight or the scope of my own imagination. I need others, many, many others, to contribute to such a vision.

Throughout this volume you will find essays describing how to build workable political coalitions, as well as others making the case for why various issues are integral to the agenda of a more politically dynamic Religious Left. It is not my intent to pile on with more examples of either. Rather, I hope to make the case that we cannot, and ought not, win if we don't build broad coalitions with visions and agendas that refuse to exclude anyone out of either expedience or blindness.

With each passing year I become more convinced that movements cannot be sustained on outrage alone. Which is a pity, for we have much to be outraged by: economic policies that protect and engorge already obscenely wealthy individuals and business interests at the expense of the poor (and the formerly middle-class who are joining them); incursions on civil liberties that target the most vulnerable in order to persuade the rest of us that our safety is being attended to; governmental attempts to regulate who we love and when, how, and if we bear children while privatizing those things government is best equipped to attend to—education, health care, the social safety net, even defense and the waging of war. Each of us could fill pages with additions to the list of the outrageous and the unconscionable.

Perhaps one of the most fundamental outrages of all is the erosion of honest public discourse. When, instead of disagreeing honestly, the Right (or any of us) practice to deceive and to cut off debate with spurious claims, whether through biased, agenda-driven (B.A.D.) science, disingenuous assertions about what the Bible purportedly says, or lies about weapons of mass destruction, we are left unable to know what to believe, how to speak in order to be heard, how to struggle together to discern truth. By all means, let us put our values and convictions on the table, with the facts, and then let's disagree about the moral and policy implications of that data. Let us disagree passionately—an indicator of how seriously we take it all. But let's disagree honestly. Otherwise, we salt the ground of civic discourse that has, through the ages, led to astonishing new discoveries as well as moral enlightenment.

We have much to be outraged by. Yet the smug satisfaction that accompanies un-tempered outrage is good neither for the health of our souls nor for the movements we strive to build and serve. Outrage, no matter how powerful, how justified, how often re-stoked, cannot survive the long haul. It burns hot, but it burns fast. To see our work through we need the steady fire of our vision to center and sustain us. This vision may, and will, take many forms as we each bring our own interests and passions to the table but, in all its forms, it must incorporate the broad reach of issues and agenda. It must link our passions.

Fortunately, linking our agendas is not difficult—it is, in fact, almost inevitable. Reproductive Justice, for example, depends not just on safe, affordable access to abortion, but also on all those things that give women and families real options—that make possible the choice to bear and raise children as well as the choice to avoid, and, when necessary, to terminate pregnancies. Therefore, we cannot talk adequately about reproductive justice without also talking about health care, child care, job security and, safety from violence. LGBTQ rights are linked to the whole spectrum of gender equity, as well as to social security, health care, immigration … and immigration is inseparable from racial justice, education, civil liberties. The links are endless if we train our eyes to see the complementarities rather than the conflicts.

The problems arise when, in the heat of pitched battles over issues closest to our heart, bedeviled by a zero-sum mentality, we too often back-burner our the concerns of our allies, or worse yet, barter them away, in an attempt to capture ground in our own fights. This not only fractures our movements, dims our vision, and gives lie to our professed values, it also too often wins us only trivial and illusory victories. For our issues truly are too tightly linked to sacrifice even one without crippling all the others. Even we ourselves, often under the same skin, carry multiple identities linked to multiple issues. The opportunities to privilege one issue, one identity, at the expense of others are constant and seductive. But they lead to death and dismemberment—requiring us to try to separate and sacrifice parts of ourselves, sacrificing the whole for the illusion of protecting one or another part. (Or as the prophet Jeremiah once found in a valley—dry bones.) Ask anyone who witnessed the 2008 Democratic presidential primaries. Look at how easily they led to fractures in the movement as leaders and activists, reluctantly sometimes but still adamantly, chose their sides—anti-racist or anti-sexist. Ask Black women for whom this false dichotomy cut particularly close to the bone. Most of us carry multiple passions; many of us also carry multiple identities. As long as we continue to fight against this or that most recent atrocity of the Right rather than for a comprehensive Progressive vision, we will be doomed to face such "Sophie's choices"—choices that promise death for most and no real life for any.

The Right has known, and acted on, this principle of linking issues under a broad vision for at least sixty years. They've made connections between their own, potentially competitive, issues while creating wedges to drive between the issues of the Left. And, too often, we on the Left have taken the bait, allowing ourselves not only to compete with one another's issues but also, even within single issues, to disdain one another's tactics. Political activists, crafting the legislation we long for, dismiss radicals in the street as unsophisticated and ineffectual. Hands on social activists, caring for the dispossessed and disregarded from within institutions or suffering communities, deride lobbyists, assuming that anyone who works within the system of political power must have been corrupted by that power. Mystics and visionaries dismiss all the rest as being too much of this world, too focused on the problems and not enough on the promise.

We fail to recognize that, as important as staunching the immediate wounds is, so, too, is changing the systems that do the wounding. As essential as political and legal work is, it requires the leverage, notice, attention that are often purchased in the rough and tumble of street demonstrations. As crucial as it is to put our bodies where our hearts are, we must have well-trained hearts with a vision worthy of our passion. In both the issues we care about and the strategies we employ, far too often, among the Left, the legs allow themselves to be convinced they have no need of the arms, the arms no need for the mouth, the mouth no need for the eyes. And so we falter, with neither vision nor victory. We allow ourselves to be divided and conquered—again and again.

Standpoint theorists and scholars of Genesis alike will know that a comprehensive vision, a vision worthy of our passion and our labor, requires a multitude of eyes. In Genesis, God's first, great gift to humankind is difference. First God creates ha-adamah (the creature of earth) containing within itself all that it means to be created in the image of God, to be human. The only thing such a creature lacked was the ability to be in relationship with; since it comprised everything of what it meant to be human, it could not encounter any "other." Seeing this irredeemable loneliness, God took that creature of earth and divided it—creating difference. Male and female, Jew and Greek, gay and straight, Democrat and Republican, every color and age and culture … in creating difference we were given the opportunity to encounter others, not to be alone in all of creation. At the same time, the reflection of the image of God within each of us was made incomplete. Those "others" contain parts of the image not in us. We need each other's vision, each other's likeness of God, to enable us to see all that is possible and desirable in this world—all that God intends human-kind to be. Or, if religious metaphor isn't your cup of tea (which is fine—we need our differences) each of us can only view reality from the perspective of our own experience—the place on which we stand. We need those who stand elsewhere to show us things we could not otherwise see, would not otherwise notice.

For practical purposes it is essential that we invite in, seek out, solicit, seduce, and search for a variety of voices from every margin, listening always for that we have not yet heard, striving always to make connections, to weave a common vision more complex and complete than any of our individual agendas could allow. Strategically, this offers our best hope of success. Morally, it offers the only success worthy of our passion.

RELIGIOUS RIGHT, RELIGIOUS LEFT

⇐

CHIP BERLET

"…the end is reconciliation; the end is redemption; the end is the creation of the beloved community." — Dr. Martin Luther King, Jr.

When I speak in public about my criticisms of the Religious Right, I often identify myself as someone who is trying to help build a Religious Left. A common response to this statement is, "Oh great, that's all we need. Now we'll have twice as many problems." I hope that is not the case, as I don't think additional problems are the likely outcome of attempts to remobilize a Religious Left in the United States.

On the contrary, I have faith that the resurgence of an authentic, politically dynamic Religious Left will be part of a new broad progressive coalition that will help fulfill the long delayed promise of American democracy for all people, especially those who have historically been oppressed, marginalized, and abandoned by our society.

Throughout our history as a nation, Religious Left activists have been fierce advocates for justice and equality and opponents of unfair concentrations of privilege and power. In addition, they have joined with secularists and civil libertarian religious conservatives to defend our Constitutional tradition of separation of church and state.

Few people realize that my activism and analysis is rooted in progressive Christian theology. As a teenager in the 1960s, I joined the Civil Rights Movement after reading the "Letter from Birmingham Jail" by the Reverend Martin Luther King, Jr.—which was used as a study guide in my Presbyterian youth group. I went on to help run a church-based coffee house in suburban New Jersey, and an ecumenical youth camp in New Hampshire. Later on, at the University of Denver, one of my mentors was the school's dean, a Presbyterian minister by the name of John Rice. (Rice is perhaps better known as the father of Condoleezza). Dean Rice taught me about institutional racism and white privilege, and as a result, in 1971 we invited him to speak at a campus rally on the anniversary of the Kent and Jackson State student killings. During his speech, Rice challenged us: "When tomorrow comes will you be the perpetuators of war or of peace? Are you the generation to bring to America a lasting peace? Or did your brothers and sisters at Kent and Jackson State die in vain?" When tomorrow came, I was arrested along with many others for committing non-violent civil disobedience at the Denver Federal Center.

I suspect that most people who are skeptical about religious or spiritual beliefs have not spent a great deal of time thinking about how the Religious Right and Religious Left differ in their goals and methods. Why is this so important? Because, on one hand, understanding how the Religious Right gained so much power in this country will assist us in constructing effective challenges to that power. And, on the other hand, knowing more about progressive religious and spiritual activists will assist secularists in the process of building respectful and durable coalitions with us in order to advance the causes of equality, peace, economic justice, and a healthy environment.

WHAT IS THE RELIGIOUS RIGHT?

"In the 1970s New Right strategists took the lead within the right by identifying white conservative Christians as potential recruits for the movement." — Jean Hardisty

The Religious Right is the common name for a series of interlocking social and political movements that were knitted together in the 1970s and gained prominence in the 1980s. For the most part, the Religious Right is composed of Christians, with a handful of traditionalists and conservatives from other religions joining in on projects where there are overlapping concerns.

Christianity in the United States is broadly divided into Catholicism and Protestantism. While the largest branch of Catholicism is the Roman Catholic Church, there are also a variety of other branches, including the Orthodox churches. Protestantism split away from Roman Catholicism in the 1500s, and is today divided into numerous denominations and independent churches. Within Protestantism, there have historically been periods of widespread revivalist mobilizations which sometimes intersect with political activism. We are in the middle of one of those moments today.

Secularism may be on the increase in the United States, but a significant majority of Americans still believe in God, and about 50 percent say they are adherents of an organized religious belief system. Depending on how the question is asked, some 25 to 45 percent of the U.S. population report that they see themselves as either "Born-Again" Christians, or, in the broadest sense of the word, Christian "evangelicals." While most mainline Protestant denominations are shrinking in size, there is substantial growth in the most demanding and orthodox Protestant churches.

We know that there really is something called the Christian Right because exit polls have found that roughly 15 percent of the voters in Presidential elections say they are allied in some way with the movement. A big mess results, however, when pollsters decide to ask about concerns over "moral values" or "family values," and think they are measuring the Christian Right. Most Americans are concerned about "moral values" or "family values," whether or not they describe themselves as religious—even those of us on the political left…even the pagans and atheists.

WHO ARE THESE FOLKS?

There are three ways to view Christian evangelicals, according to the Institute for the Study of American Evangelicals (ISAE): as people of faith that follow a set of specific doctrines; as an organic network of traditions; or as a self-identified religious coalition that emerged during World War II.

When viewed as an organic network of traditions, ISAE explains that evangelicalism "denotes a style as much as a set of beliefs. As a result, groups as disparate as black Baptists and Dutch Reformed Churches, Mennonites and Pentecostals, Catholic charismatics and Southern Baptists all come under the evangelical umbrella—demonstrating just how diverse the movement really is."

Core evangelical doctrines, according to historian David Bebbington, are the belief in the need to change lives through conversion; expressing the message of the gospels through activism; a strong regard for the Bible as a guide for life; and stressing the importance of Christ's sacrifice on the cross.

The terms Fundamentalist, Born-Again, Pentecostal, and Charismatic denote specific and sometimes overlapping stylistic subsets of Christianity, and primarily are found within Protestant evangelicalism. To be Born-Again implies a personal religious conversion experience that involves a powerful sense of being imbued with the spirit of God. Pentecostals and Charismatics believe that they routinely manifest gifts from the Holy Spirit such as speaking in tongues or being swept up into physical ecstasy by the Lord of the Dance.

Fundamentalists read the Bible literally, reject liberal church doctrine, and tend to shun secular society. "A fundamentalist is an evangelical who is angry about something" quips historian George Marsden. In the late 1800s, a split began within Protestantism over what was denounced as the accommodation by leaders of the Methodists, Presbyterians, Lutherans, (and other major denominations) of the scientific method—particularly Darwin's theory of evolution. In addition, these folks were suspicious of educational reform movements developed by John Dewey, and troubled by the ideas of new immigrants and new lifestyles—which back then meant the eight hour work day and women wearing pants. I like to think of it as the 3-D effect—Darwin, Dewey, and Diversity.

By the 1920s, a group of ministers and theologians had issued a list of "fundamental" religious beliefs to which they thought every Christian should adhere. These fundamental beliefs not only excluded the teachings of the Roman Catholic Church, but the "mainline" Protestant denominations as well. The Scopes "Monkey Trial" of 1925 highlighted this split in popular culture, as the State of Tennessee fired John Scopes for teaching evolution rather than the Biblical story of creation. While creationism won in court, fundamentalism were so ridiculed in the media that many in the movement retreated from public political participation for several decades.

While the fundamentalists went underground, other conservative Christians remained politically active. In particular, the views of what historian Leo Ribuffo calls the "Old Christian Right," a collection of strident demagogues often surfing a subtext of white supremacy and anti-Semitism, resonated across much of society in the 1930s.

THE CHRISTIAN RIGHT AND POLITICAL POWER

With the election of Franklin D. Roosevelt, a broad range of conservative Christians worried that government and labor union "collectivism" threatened the social contract, the radical individualism of unrefined Calvinism, and the proper relationship between the Godly individual and the church and the state. As a result, "Big Government" and "Big Labor" were attacked as anti-Christian, as well as greasing the skids down the slippery slope toward Godless socialism and eventually Communist tyranny. As rightist economist Friedrich A. Hayek put it in the title of his 1944 book, America was on *The Road to Serfdom*. Underlying all of this was a version of Calvinist dogma and economic free market thinking that sociologist Max Weber called "The Protestant Ethic and the Spirit of Capitalism."

After the Second World War, industrial capitalism grew alongside Calvinism and a symbiotic relationship developed. According to sociologist Sara Diamond, early Calvinists "justified their accumulation of wealth, even at the expense of others, on the grounds that they were somehow destined to prosper. It is no surprise that such notions still find resonance within the Christian Right."

The post WWII development of Cold War ideology—especially anti-communism—helped to bring some fundamentalists back into the public sphere. During this period, William F. Buckley, Jr. and his cohorts forged a political coalition that united conservative Christians, social traditionalists, anticommunists, anti-union activists, corporate fat cats, and right-wing economic libertarians. While these sectors all had different ideologies and strategic goals, they were able to work together around common tactical interests. The Christian Right of this period was allied with and funded by major corporate interests, and thus had a more sophisticated approach than the Old Christian Right.

During the 1950s and 1960s, what became known as the evangelical movement attracted people from both fundamentalist churches and mainline denominations, cutting across many theological and political boundaries. Evangelist Billy Graham sought to energize evangelicals and fundamentalists in the 1950s through a spiritual revival, as well as trying to build a renewal movement within the mainline denominations. In part, this was done to create a bulwark against the threat of external communist military power and what was seen as widespread internal subversion by communists, socialists, and their "parlor pink" liberal allies. Some of the activists, including Phyllis Schlafly, sought to take over the Republican Party. However, the defeat of conservative Republican Presidential candidate Barry Goldwater in 1964 sent these right-wing activists back to the drawing board.

In 1976, Democrat Jimmy Carter (a professing Baptist evangelical) was elected President with the enthusiastic support of many previously non-voting or Republican voting evangelicals. It was a rude shock, therefore, when President Carter's IRS sent out letters to hundreds of segregated white Christian private schools, threatening to terminate their non-profit tax status. Historian Randall Balmer, an evangelical critic of the Christian Right, has documented how this threat sparked a mass mobilization of evangelical activists who became involved in public policy and political struggles.

It was these newly engaged white conservative evangelical Christian voters who propelled Republican Ronald Reagan into office in 1980. While Reagan never delivered on his promises to end abortion and restore prayer in schools, he did begin to involve Christian Right leaders in policy formation, and appointed their acolytes to federal agencies.

After Christian Right televangelist Pat Robertson ran a failed 1988 campaign for the Republican presidential nod, he converted his campaign operation into the Christian Coalition, which began to issue biased voter guides and became a leading Christian Right national network during the administration of George H.W. Bush.

In the 1990s, the Christian Coalition joined a network of

conservative groups in launching political attacks on President Bill Clinton, whose second term as president was sidetracked by lurid tales of sexual peccadilloes and conspiracy theories about financial skullduggery and the assassination of political allies turned political liabilities.

The Christian Right truly found its voice in 2000. One study found that 40 percent of the total vote for George W. Bush in the 2000 election came from Christian evangelicals, making it the largest single voting bloc in the Republican Party. Seventy-nine percent of evangelicals who voted for Bush in 2000 had been contacted at least once by a politicized religious group or individual, as compared to 36 percent of Gore voters. Despite this, many evangelicals have long been "swing voters" oscillating between the Republican and Democratic Parties; and many more simply feel neither Party represents their interests. In 2004 a small yet significant number of White evangelicals switched to vote Democratic, primarily due to concerns over Republican political corruption and the war in Iraq.

Today, the Family Research Council, which replaced the Christian Coalition as the leading national network for the Christian Right, hosts Values Voters Washington Briefings in the nation's capital to mobilize evangelical leaders to build grassroots support for conservative candidates. Neither the Democrats nor progressive social movement organizations have anything close to the Christian Right's complex national structure for organizing voters.

DIFFERENT STROKES

"Let justice roll down like waters, and righteousness like an everflowing stream ..."— The Prophet Amos

What does it mean to be part of the Christian Left? I can only speak for myself, but I see distinct differences between a progressive Christian worldview and the views of most leaders of the Christian

Right. Here are some of my yardsticks for measuring the differences between the Christian Right and Christian Left.

RELIGIOUS BELIEF: TRIUMPHALIST OR PLURALIST?

A few years ago I was invited to a national conference of relatively conservative evangelicals to talk about how some Christians use specific apocalyptic readings of Biblical text to justify demonizing other people and groups. These folks felt this was a problem and wanted to know more about how to resist these tendencies. After my presentation, an audience member politely asked me what I thought of the fact that most of the attendees believed the only way to heaven was through accepting Jesus Christ as lord and savior—so that only Christians can be saved from eternal death.

The preacher from the host church, next to me at the podium, touched my arm and stepped forward. "I know what our churches teach," he said, "and I am not going to challenge it." Then he paused, "but if God let's everyone into heaven, if everyone is saved, would that be such a bad thing?" In his elegant answer, the preacher demonstrated how humility can honor specific orthodox religious beliefs while creating space for democratic pluralism. His was a way to expand the circle of those seeking justice, not shrink it.

When a religious leader insists that it is "my way or the highway" (to Hell), that attitude is called "Triumphalism." In Christianity, triumphalism has been the driving forces the Crusades and the Inquisition, as well as fostering numerous wars, purges, witch hunts, and the persecution of dissidents labeled "heretics."

Partly in response to this grim history, the U.S. Constitution was designed to promote a pluralist society, where people can choose to have or reject religious beliefs, and change their minds about these things free from the undue influence of government or powerful religious institutions. The Bill of Rights starts out with the mandate that "Congress shall make no law respecting an establishment of religion, or prohibiting the free exercise thereof." The Religious Left that I am helping build is one that defends pluralism against triumphalism, as we see pluralism as a core value of democratic civil society.

GOVERNMENT: DOMINIONISM OR SEPARATION?

"Dominionism" is a tendency among Protestant Christian evangelicals and fundamentalists that encourages not only active political participation in civic matters, but also seeks to dominate the political process, all as part of a mandate from God. The Christian Right's road to political power is paved with the tenets of dominionism. This highly politicized concept is based on Genesis 1:26:

> "And God said, Let us make man in our image, after our likeness: and let them have dominion over the fish of the sea, and over the fowl of the air, and over the cattle, and over all the earth, and over every creeping thing that creepeth upon the earth."

Most Christians read this and conclude that God has appointed humans as stewards and caretakers of the Earth. Some Christians however believe, as Sara Diamond explains, "that Christians alone are Biblically mandated to occupy all secular institutions until Christ returns—and there is no consensus on when that might be." That, in a nutshell, is the idea of "dominionism." In *The Public Eye*, Frederick Clarkson identifies the commonalities across the range of dominionist ideas:

> Dominionists celebrate *Christian nationalism*, in that they believe that the United States once was, and should once again be, a Christian nation. In this way, they deny the Enlightenment roots of American democracy.

Dominionists promote *religious supremacy*, insofar as they generally do not respect the equality of other religions, or even other versions of Christianity.

Dominionists endorse *theocratic visions*, insofar as they believe that the Ten Commandments, or "biblical law," should be the foundation of American law, and that the U.S. Constitution should be seen as a vehicle for implementing Biblical principles.

Some liberal authors warn that most conservative Christian evangelicals desire a fascistic Christian Nationalist Theocracy, like that outlined by hardcore Dominion Theology movements such as Christian Reconstructionism. That's like suggesting that all vegetarians want to round up and execute meat-eaters.

SACRED TEXT: MARCHING ORDERS OR STUDY GUIDE?

For over a century, Baptists in the United States prided themselves on the belief that each individual was empowered to read the Bible independently, and to interpret the sacred text in his or her own way. This view began to change when authoritarian ultraconservatives took over the Southern Baptist Convention in the 1970s and began issuing ultimatums banning women as preachers and stigmatizing a growing enemies list that included gay people, reproductive rights advocates, political liberals, and even Freemasons.

However, what if all sacred text is the inspired word of God, imperfectly understood and transposed by imperfect human beings? Then the point is to use the text as a study guide for trying to imagine the possibilities and our obligations to those possibilities. The Religious Left I am part of is composed of folks seeking the truth, but never so arrogant as to believe that they speak for God. We certainly don't use our sacred texts to justify oppression.

Dr. Peter J. Gomes, minister at The Memorial Church at Harvard University, argues that the Bible must be read carefully to avoid using the text to legitimize "doctrinaire prejudices" in the dominant culture. In *The Good Book: Reading the Bible with Heart and Mind,* Gomes suggests Biblical literacy as an antidote to Biblical literalism.

RELIGION: EMPIRE OR LIBERATION?

Ruby Sales is the founder of Spirit House in Washington, D.C. In the 1960s, she joined the Civil Rights movement while a student at Tuskegee University in Alabama. After becoming involved in the Student Non-Violent Coordinating Committee, Sales was arrested in 1965 along other activists for protesting against segregation and conducting a voter registration drive. Upon her release from jail, Sales and her colleagues were confronted by an enraged white racist wielding a shotgun. To her horror, Sales saw her organizing colleague and friend Jonathan Daniels, a White Episcopalian seminary student, shot to death on the street after he pushed her out of harm's way. The trauma left Sales speechless for seven months, but she persevered, found her voice, and carried on with her activism, eventually attending the same divinity school where Daniels had studied. Today, Sales continues to struggle for justice, tempered with compassion.

After the demoralizing 2004 re-election of George W. Bush, I spent several days with Sales and other activists. We talked about how we are mandated by our spiritual beliefs to stand up and speak out in support of justice, and how we all have to choose sides in the endless struggle. Are we on the side of the powerful, the arrogant, the bullies who seek empire? Or are we on the side of the weak, the impoverished, the marginalized, seeking liberation for those who are suffering under the weight of oppression?

Sales placed the unsettling 2004 elections in the context of a historic struggle within Christianity:

> The Empire religion espoused by George Bush and his white Christian conservative allies is headed by a God who appears to be white supremacist, patriarchal, and upper class, one who stands on the side of enslavement and the genocide of native peoples throughout the globe.

> This is the message of conservative right-wing Christians, who misuse scripture to justify their beliefs, and hide their intentions behind self-centered and pious God talk that undergirds and propels exclusion and domination— whether about the inferiority of women, black people, or lesbians and gays.

> Liberation Christianity begins with the assertion that God is on the side of the oppressed rather than the side of the Empire. This was the belief of a radical Jew named Jesus, who challenged the Roman Empire.

Empire Christianity is based on oppression. My version of progressive Christianity sees sin as the will to oppress. Therefore, one of the ways in which we overcome sin is by opposing empire and working for the liberation of all people from empires, small and large.

APOCALYPTIC PROPHECY: GUERILLA WAR OR REDEMPTIVE PEACE?

Christianity, Judaism, and Islam all draw from apocalyptic traditions that date back thousands of years. The words apocalypse, prophecy, and revelation come from the same linguistic roots; today, the concept means the belief in an approaching confrontation representing a struggle between good and evil during which hidden truths will be revealed, after which society will be transformed.

For fundamentalists such as Tim LaHaye and John Hagee, the apocalypse involves a global battle between Godly Christians and agents of Satan that will begin in the Middle East, follow by the return of Jesus to the Temple Mount in Jerusalem. Then, unless we all confess our sins and embrace Jesus, we will be gathered together and slaughtered by an angry God. The method of execution is a gigantic wine press that crushes us until our blood flows in a gushing river through the valley of Megiddo in Israel. Thus, the grapes of wrath. The cosmic hit list is long, and includes not just heretical or flawed Christians, but also secular humanists, Godless liberals, reproductive rights advocates, gay men, lesbians, Muslims, Hindus, and most Jews (except for the 144,000 who convert to Christianity in the nick of time, according to one literal reading of sacred Biblical text).

Brenda E. Brasher, a sociologist of religion, explains that "Apocalypticism is potentially beneficent or potentially destructive" and what helps determine the outcome is how the "person or group or idea being confronted" is constructed. Brasher explains that this depends on the "definition of the status of the 'Other' in the anticipated confrontation. If the 'other' is constructed as wholly evil, then the ramifications are really horrendous." According to Brasher, in this negative dualistic form:

> Apocalypticism leaves no room for ambiguity in the stories told about the "Other." There is a real hardening of sides. We are good, they are evil. This is not a disagreement, but a struggle with evil incarnate, so there is no structure for a peaceful reconciliation.

> People are cast in their roles as either enemy or friend and

there is no middle ground. In the battle with evil, can you really say you are neutral?

In contrast to this worldview, the apocalyptic tradition of many African American evangelicals is far more positive and hopeful, rooted in the idea that the apocalypse will bring justice. One interpretation is that there will come a day when white Christians will confess the sin of racism and are forgiven and redeemed. This was the prophetic tradition of the Reverend Martin Luther King, Jr.

MAKING PROGRESS

"Pray for the dead and fight like hell for the living." — Mother Jones

For many of us on the Christian Left, the inevitable apocalyptic confrontation is not a bloody guerrilla war, but the necessity of speaking truth to power, challenging the status quo, and thus transforming society. Our vision of prophecy leads us to seek the Beloved Community. For those of us challenging the Christian Right, the issue is not secular versus spiritual ideologies; the issue is how to craft a pluralist civil society that honors the dignity of both secular philosophy and spiritual faith—while insisting that theological claims alone should never dictate public policy. That is why we say we are challenging theocracy, because that is what the Christian Right leadership is increasingly sowing: a theocratic society.

Stereotyping all conservative evangelicals as a bunch of theocratic fascists, however, is counterproductive histrionics. Most evangelicals don't want tyranny, and many have been involved for decades in movements to protect the environment, end the arms race, seek peace, alleviate poverty, develop compassionate policies for health care and housing needs, and support a living wage for working people. Reports that these are new trends or irresolvable wedge issues signaling the imminent collapse of the Christian

Right are ahistorical and absurd.

It is also counterproductive to denounce religion itself as the problem. Setting aside the historic reality that secular totalitarians have been just as bloodthirsty and brutal as religious totalitarians, there is the obvious practical issue that in a society where the vast majority of residents believe in God, no sensible and serious organizer is going to get very far denouncing religion. I work with plenty of secularists and agnostics, and while we happily debate religion and faith over a beer, when we are out in public as organizers, we set those differences aside so that we can build a broad coalition. Simply put, progressive need to learn how to work in alliance with people of faith.

Loretta Ross is the National Coordinator of the SisterSong Women of Color Reproductive Health Collective in Atlanta, Georgia. She is adamant that if we want to build a truly progressive human rights movement, the "secular left and the religious left need each other," but, at the same time, we "don't need to pull each other to our particular point of view" on matters involving faith. People can maintain their own beliefs, while coming to understand that "real allies need each other in ways that are not patronizing or disrespectful," Ross says. "As organizers, we need to understand and enthusiastically support the need for people to have rituals and beliefs just like we want others to respect ours. It is kind of hard to persuade people you hold in contempt. We need to learn how to respect and embrace differences among people moving in the same direction."

Across town, the Reverend Timothy McDonald, pastor of the First Iconium Baptist Church, explains that in the Black community, "it is almost expected that an independent Black pastor is engaged and involved in some way and some form with human rights and civil rights struggles." McDonald is a national leader in these arenas, as are many Black pastors and parishioners. Yet many White organizers are still reluctant to join coalitions with religious people of color. As a progressive, when I look for ideas from people of faith, I look to many different voices and beliefs, including the Reverend Carlton Veazey, President of the Religious Coalition for Reproductive Choice; Rabbi David Saperstein, Director of the Religious Action Center of Reform Judaism; the Reverend Susan Brooks Thistlethwaite, president of Chicago Theological Seminary; Mohammad Ja`far Mahallati of the Ilex Foundation, and Pastor Dan Schultz of the online community *Street Prophets*. On a personal level, I turn to friends with whom I share communion, including the Reverend Denise Griebler, a United Church of Christ minister in Illinois, and Dart Westphal, a community organizer, environmental activist, and lay leader at the evangelical Lutheran Church of the Epiphany in the Bronx.

As a movement, the Religious Left is a work in progress. However, just think about how powerful it would be to build a broad coalition based on a shared commitment to craft a democracy that really works, and in which all people are full members. Where oppression, supremacy, and greed are denounced as uncivilized?

Building such a movement is hard work. Bernice Johnson Reagon, an activist, scholar, and performer, appreciates the difficulty of building diverse and democratic coalitions. Attending a 1981 meeting of women held at a high altitude national park, Reagon found herself having difficulty breathing. In that she sees a parallel to building powerful coalitions. "I feel as if I'm gonna keel over any minute and die. That is often what it feels like if you're really doing coalition work. Most of the time you feel threatened to the core and if you don't, you're not really doing no coalescing."

As progressives, let us agree to disagree on the issue of spiritual belief. There are so many other matters on which we can wholeheartedly agree. It's time to take a risk and do some real coalescing. As we enter a new phase of the struggle for basic human rights, the chances of success will be greatly enhanced if we learn how to bridge divides of race, class, gender, sexual identity, and personal beliefs that range from secular to religious.

In the mid 1990s, I worked with human rights activists Loretta Ross and Suzanne Pharr to gather together a circle of progressive strategists to evaluate our work as national organizers and researchers. We did so with a real sense of humility. Our failures and missteps were many. Following three days of heartfelt discussion and candid self-criticism, we wrote "A Call to Defend Democracy and Pluralism." Here is how we ended our essay:

> The leaders of the anti-democratic right say their movement is waging a battle for the soul of America. They call it a culture war. We believe the soul of America should not be a battleground but a birthright, and that culture should be celebrated not censored. We believe America is defined by ideas and values, but not those limited by religious beliefs, biology, bloodlines, or birthplace of ancestors. The time has come to stand up and vigorously defend democracy and pluralism against the attacks orchestrated by cynical leaders of the anti-democratic right. History teaches us that there can be no freedom without liberty, no liberty without justice, and no justice without equality; and we look forward to success because we know it is through the never-ending struggle for equality, justice, liberty and freedom that democracy is nourished.

Today, I see young organizers stepping up to the challenge of rebuilding a truly democratic and diverse progressive movement for social change. I have great hope for the future as these activists assume leadership roles. Ultimately, I see us all as links in a chain of the struggle for justice that stretches back before recorded history and reaches forward into the future.

Who's God?
Faith, Democracy, and the
Making of an Authentic
Religious Left

⇐

REV. OSAGYEFO UHURU SEKOU

It seemed that both god and democracy had failed. How could a nation that claimed to be a democracy abandon the citizens of New Orleans? Why would god allow some of the poorest people in the nation to be swept away?

As the post Katrina horrors unfolded before me, I was plagued by these questions of political angst. In addition, I was also experiencing a profound crisis of faith. I had moved to New Orleans to serve as founding Executive Director of the Interfaith Worker Justice Center of New Orleans. When I arrived a year and half after Katrina hit, I found a city in total disrepair, with few signs of organized success towards rebuilding.

I lived in Algiers on the West Bank of the Mississippi River. Each day, at around 7:30 in the morning, I would leave my four room shotgun house and walk to the neighborhood cafe, Tout de Suite, responding along the way to several patrons singing, "Good morning, Reverend." I would grab a stool at the coffee bar, drank a double cappuccino, and depart to a similar serenade, "Have a good day, Reverend."

Hearing people call me Reverend often sent a chill up my spine, because most days I no longer believed in god. New Orleans had broken something in me. The images of folks stranded on rooftops and packed in the Superdome are the lenses through which I still look for god and for the promise of democracy in America. New Orleans is a phenomenon. It is the birthplace of jazz—America's first original art form—as well as being an extraordinary mix of cultures, reflected in the city's food, architecture, skin tones, and social life. Yet it is also the site of this country's greatest disaster (both natural and human-made). The birthplace of jazz is now the death bed of democracy.

As I walked through the elegantly dressed streets of Old Algiers Point, I was amused by gawking small children in their strollers. Eventually, I would arrive at the west bank ferry dock, sitting down and smoking my pipe while gazing out at the muddy waters of the Mississippi. A few minutes later, boarding the ferry for the magical ride across the river, I would notice that my fellow ferry travelers were an eclectic mix of artists, anarchists, immigrants and exiles. I was struck most by those who wore maid and maintenance uniforms. These men and women spoke with a unique musicality. Their term of endearment for one another—"baby"—was elongated and tuned in a minor key that would have made Louis Armstrong smile. But I cried. I cried everyday because their misery was tangible.

Upon arriving on the east bank, the ferry would dock at the edge of downtown, near the hotels and casinos. My fellow passengers were headed to what author Douglas Coupland called "McJobs"—low wage, low prestige, non-benefited work. In a city whose economy centers on tourism, there is only one union hotel. I would then board a street car to our offices.

The unwritten part of my job description often called for me to conduct "devastation" tours for academics and activists who were visiting the city. They always requested to go to the ground zero of the greatest man made disaster in this nation's history-the Lower Ninth Ward. For miles, homes were torn from their foundations, democracy cracked to its core. One was overcome with a deep sense of sadness. Silence filled the air. Hope choked. As our minivan crawled through the devastation, we would see the tour buses gawking at the misery of the poor of New Orleans.

I would always point out to those with me that some of the houses were signed with an odd signature. It was not the infamous X with codes in each quadrant to signify the name of the unit that had searched the residence, its location, date of inspection, and the number of dead (humans and animals) inside. Instead, these houses simply read, "Baghdad." "Baghdad on the bayou," I thought, aloud.

On one tour, we crossed back over the St. Cloud Street Bridge and saw a National Guard Humvee in the parking lot of a McDonald's. Moments later, several Guardsmen emerged—machine guns in hand—escorting two Black teenagers out in handcuffs. I later learned that National Guard personnel retain their weapons during their different deployments, and that most of the Guard troops in New Orleans had been redeployed from Iraq. As a result, the same guns that were used to "establish democracy" in Iraq were being used by members of the National Guard to secure the city of New Orleans.

IMPERIAL GOD

I spent a lot of time alone, looking for a way out of my crisis of faith. Where was my god in the midst of all this misery? I turned on the television and watched a lot of cable news. There was a god there, but it was one that I did not know. From divining the war in Iraq to Jerry Farewell's proclamation that Katrina was god's wrath visited upon America for its tolerance of gays and other "deviant" behavior, this god had been strategically employed by the powerful to divide the electorate and impose restrictions on democratic opportunity. This god maintained a hegemony over our public discourse; a supreme being that was synonymous with empire and its economy—an imperial god. Consider that for some years one has been able to interchange the words "Christian," "conservative," "religious," "right," and "Republican" in one sentence without necessarily changing the meaning of the sentence. A lexicon shift of this magnitude is an indication of profound meaning-making power. The god I was seeing on television was the chief force driving the constriction of democratic opportunity in the U.S. and the taking of democracy's name in vain abroad.

After six months in New Orleans in the face of the astounding misery that confronted so many there, and a twenty-four hour electronic barrage from the imperial god, I had to ask myself: "How can you believe in god?" A god that launched a pre-emptive war and punished the most vulnerable was a god I wanted no part of. A religion that defended the powerful over the powerless was not my religion.

NEO-LIBERAL GOD

In light of my personal crisis of faith and the global exploitation of religion, I have come to believe that nothing less than an epistemic break on the magnitude of the founding of Christianity and the depth of the Protestant Reformation will save our democracy. What has emerged over the last two decades is not a break, but a theological capitulation to the neo-liberal economy by religious and non-religious folks alike.

For most, religion is a meaning-making activity. We humans use it to situate ourselves within a broader context in the face of dread, death, and despair because it offers us an eternal story when we are comforted with a finite reality. Given that the critical victory of the Right has been existential rather than political, any countervailing project must highlight the existential. This intervention is critical to our understanding the way in which we derive meaning. To achieve such an aim, we must—as Cornel West often notes—take an ontological risk that will lead to existential vertigo. What is at stake is how we make meaning for ourselves within the dual languages of religion and democracy. This must therefore be a central part of the task of re-visioning a Religious Left. And it will require great theological, spiritual, and political courage on our part.

Unfortunately, what has been taken by many to be an adequate popular countervailing religious argument is not up to the meaning-making task that is at hand. However, it does let us glimpse what we might call the neo-liberal god. By the neo-liberal god, I am referring to a religious movement in contemporary politics that has absorbed as its own the framework and policies of neo-liberalism. In the same manner in which the religious right has sanctified the imperial aims of the Bush Administration, neo-liberal religious leaders have adopted the policy stances that bless neo-liberal political policies, which includes free trade, welfare reform, personal responsibility, and privatization of social services. These policies born out of the neoliberal discourse provide the "talking" points for many religious leaders on the left.

The most popular books written by an ostensibly liberal religious leader are *God's Politics* and *The Great Awakening*. Both books attack the supposed lack of religious sensibility on the political left and the religious right's monopoly on god-talk in the marketplace. Both have reached the *New York Times* Bestseller list, and the books' author, Jim Wallis, speaks to sold-out audiences around the country. Despite his popularity, Wallis and his Sojourners/Call to Renewal organization do not engage or take seriously the discourse of those it claims to serve—i.e. the poor—a discourse which is best embodied by the radical tradition of African-American religion. Wallis' inability to claim the radical politics of the prophetic tradition serves to undermine the stated mission of his work, thereby limiting his capacity to articulate the development of an authentic Religious Left. Indeed, Wallis publicly argues against the organization of a Religious Left, arguing instead for a "moral center." While supporting a neo-liberal politic, Wallis often makes simplistic references to the prophetic tradition of the Black church—which reshaped the meaning of democracy by including those who had been historically "othered." Unfortunately, Wallis does not actually listen to this tradition.

Equally, his frequent claim that the Religious Right is dead is not only incorrect—it is dangerous. The Religious Right has defined two of the most fundamental activities of meaning making in human ecology-religion and politics. They have set the terms of the discourse in which all political discourse currently responds. We are unable to experience a radical break from this frame because the neo-liberal project merely changes the words, not the language. While *God's Politics* devotes a lot of space to teaching the Democratic Party how to be better at courting religious voters, placing religion in the service of a political party is inappropriate, if not idolatrous. Wallis is concerned with developing new religious forces and claiming the mantle of promoting social justice. But how can he do this while largely ignoring one of the richest histories of social justice in the history of our nation—the Black church? I would go so far as to say that his misguided, unfair and divisive critique of the left serves not the poor and the greater good, but instead unintentionally enables the right and its efforts to roll back the gains of the Civil Rights Movement and a century of social progress.

Despite this, Wallis has rightly identified that the younger generation hungers for social justice and spirituality. And, the success of his books may be fairly attributed to a widespread hunger for an alternative vision of religion and its role in politics.

This is the point at which I think we engage the possibility of a shift of such magnitude that an authentic Religious Left may find its heart, its head, its spirit and its voice. This is where I believe we have to go deeper, in order to set aside these essentially neoliberal tracts that smooth over the rough edges, but don't fundamentally challenge the neoliberal god, which emphasized charity over justice in New Orleans; the god whose blue light flickers in the windows of the American night. And this is where we have to take a profound ontological risk, and confront our spiritual hunger, a hunger which requires us to reject the neoliberal god that gave us the devastation of New Orleans.

The hope for an authentic Religious Left that can salvage our democracy lies in the genius and remarkable theological sophistication of African-American slaves. I believe their wisdom can serve as a guiding light to see us through the contemporary debates about religion and democracy. To begin among the poor and forgotten is both prophetic and revolutionary.

This essay is born out of my efforts to emerge from a personal crisis of faith, a crisis I saw reflected around me in the devastation of the Ninth Ward and the seeming nonchalance of much of our largely ineffectual response. I found my own way out via the community which birthed me. There I found what I pray others will find as well—the course for the healing of democracy. History bears witness that the prophetic African American religious tradition that led me out of my despair also offers hope and possibility for the nation. We stand in the river of a great tradition whose flow can carry us to greater outpourings of social justice.

This essay makes two essentialist claims. First, that the black theological project is left-of-center. It begins, historically, with the humanity of black people inside the American empire, and the worship of the prophetic god, which is a left of center claim. Secondly, that the African-American religious tradition has always read the biblical narrative in close proximity to the nation's founding documents—the Constitution and Declaration of Independence. These two streams that flow through our history and inform our contemporary discourse pose two fundamental questions: How have those who have been denied meaning made meaning of god and democracy? And, what can they teach us about our contemporary crisis?

My answers to these questions necessarily begins with my story, and how I joined in the prophetic tradition of the African American church.

THE GOD OF MY GRANDPARENTS

If Jesus is the author of my faith, then my grandparents were the editors. In rural Arkansas, I was raised in the ways of a Victorian, southern black woman who loved Jesus and justice. My grandmother, a proud Baptist, rescued me as a six-month-old from a fate that may have been too terrible to tell. A King James Bible and encyclopedias were my first gifts of memory. Later, my grandmother's admonishments, shaped by her god, posited existential gems that pointed to the measure of one's humanity: "You must never look down on people."

My grandfather, Reverend James Thomas, was a railroad worker and retired Pentecostal pastor. He possessed a third-grade education and yet was also possessed by a thirst for knowledge. He especially delighted in tidbits of black history that he had gleaned from folklore. The Bible was the book that he sought to master, and his greatest desire for me was that I also master that text in the struggle for justice. My grandfather may have only had a third-grade education, but he articulated a vision of the world that was profound.

The most magical memory I have of my granddaddy "rightly dividing the word" was on a Friday evening, after the only factory in our town had closed. With the community's economic vitality in question, granddaddy, black and burly, broad-nosed and big-lipped, stood at the sacred desk, looking out upon the sea of black and nearly broken faces. He "took" a text, as the congregation stood, the custom during the reading of scripture. Slowly and deliberately, he solicited, "If you will turn with me in your "Biiible..."—stretching the word to stress its significance—"to the gospel of John, the eleventh chapter and the thirty-fifth verse. When you find it, why don't you say, 'Amen.'"

"Amen," they responded, with great anticipation on their lips and even greater trepidation in their hearts. My granddaddy then whispered, in a tear-soaked voice, "And it simply, reads 'Jesus wept.'" Then, in the presence of a voiceless people, he made the book "talk," retelling the familiar story of Lazarus, where Jesus pleaded with his god to raise Lazarus so that others might believe. For over an hour, my granddaddy reminded a people that had been historically alienated, and were now demoralized and insecure, that they were the ones whom Jesus loved. Seamlessly blending Jesus' people's plight with the African-American struggle for freedom, my granddaddy's love for his people and the Bible merged in a way that was life affirming, and which rendered a hopeless town hopeful.

The signs, symbols, songs, and stories bequeathed to me in rural Arkansas resonated with powerful notions of justice for the poor, democracy for all, and god's desire for human freedom. Folks who were just two-and-a-half generations from slavery and functionally illiterate taught me the profundity of democracy and religion. Among them was Mrs. Roberta. On documents that required her signature, Mrs. Roberta made her mark—an X—because she could not write her name. "Come here and read to me, boy," she would command with her hands on her walking cane and royalty in her voice. "Come here, boy, and read to me about our people." I obliged, with reverence.

In the singing, prayers, testimony, and other liturgical expressions of my youthful worshipping community, Jesus was hope in hopeless circumstances. Set against the darkness, Jesus and his god were the light. In the midst of what W.E.B DuBois termed the "frenzy," they shouted Jesus is "a bright and morning star," "water in dry places," "the lily of the valley," "the rose of Sharon," "a friend to the friendless," "a rock in a weary land," "a lawyer in the court," "a doctor in the sickroom," and a whole host of phrases that formed the essence of their belief in and about the divine and their situation, which began with an assumption of their worth and redemption. They knew that the darkness would not have the last word because god was with them. My grandfather's hopes, my grandmother's vision, and Mrs. Roberta's desires all flowed from a peculiar conception of god and democracy.

Called upon during the terrible night of slavery, the prophetic god told them to "tell ol' Pharaoh to let my people go." Their unsupervised and at times contested gatherings were a counter-hegemonic practice in and of itself. A people who had been historically denied access to the broader democratic project, and ultimately their humanity, affirmed their beauty, intelligence, and capacity while praying and working out their spiritual salvation and social freedom:

> We used to slip off in the de woods in de old slave days on Sunday evening way down in de swamps to sing and pray to our own liking. We prayed for dis day of freedom. We come from four and five miles away to pray together to God dat if we don't live to see it, do please let our chillun live to see a better day and be free, so dat dey can give honest and fair service to de Lord and all mankind everywhere.

The slaves did not leave a dense theological treatise to articulate their notions of power and freedom, because it was a criminal act for slaves to learn how to read. Thus, the permissible activity of singing was their first theological text. Ex-slave Vinnie Brunson recalled, "Dey sing 'bout de joys in de nex' world an de trouble in dis. Dey first jes sung de 'ligious songs, den dey commenced to sing 'bout de life here an w'en dey sang of bof' dey called dem de 'Spirituals.'"

Reflecting death, misery, suffering, judgment, sadness, and hope, the spirituals served to articulate their situation and offer a sense of hope beyond their tragic circumstances. Oft times, the spirituals had dual meanings:

> Swing Low, Sweet Chariot,
> Coming fo' to carry me home.
> Swing Low, Sweet Chariot,
> Coming fo' to carry me home.
> Well, I looked over Jordan and what did I see,
> Coming fo' to carry me home?
> A band of angels coming after me,
> Coming fo' to carry me home

Lyrically, this song is a telling of the story of the prophetic god's entering into human history to take a faithful servant to paradise for reward, and an eschatological hope beyond the misery of the plantation. However, it was also sung as a signal that the Underground Railroad was near and that those who desired the reward of freedom on this side of the Jordan should get on board. And unlike the slave master's imperial god, their god deemed them worthy.

With this in mind, a number of African-American religious individuals, institutions, and organizations worked to end the vicious system of slavery and expand democratic opportunity for themselves and their fellow citizens. A former slave named Isabelle Baumfree believed that that god changed her name to Sojourner Truth so that she could go about preaching the good news of freedom:

> My name was Isabella; but when I left the house of bondage, I left everything behind. I wa'n't goin' to keep nothin' of Egypt on me, an' so I went to the Lord an' asked him

to give me a new name. And the Lord gave me Sojourner, because I was a travel up an' down the land, showin' the people their sins, an' bein' a sign unto them. Afterward I told the lord I wanted another name, 'cause everybody else had two names; and the Lord gave me Truth, because I was to declare the truth to the people.

Sojourner Truth also breathed theological life into America's primary founding documents, the Declaration of Independence and the Constitution:

Children, I talks to God and Gods talks to me. I goes out and talks to God in de fields and de woods. [The weevil had destroyed thousands of acres of wheat in the West that year.] Dis morning I was walking out, and I got over de fence. I saw de wheat a holding up its head, looking very big. I goes up and take holt ob it. You b'lieve it, dere was no wheat dare? I says 'God . . . , what is de matter wid dis wheat? and he says to me, "Sojourner, dere is a little weasel in it." Now I hears talkin' about de Constitution and de rights of man. I comes up and I takes hold of dis Constitution. It looks mighty big, and I feels for my rights, but der aint any dare. Den I says, God what ails dis Constitution? He says to me, "Sojourner, dere is a little weasel in it.

Harriet Tubman, the most successful conductor of the Underground Railroad, was called the Black Moses. She called upon her god to provide her with the strength to carry out the divine task of liberating others from the horrors of slavery:

I had crossed the line. I was free, but there was no one to welcome me to the land of freedom. I was a stranger in a strange land; and my home, after all, was down in Maryland; because my father, my mother, my brothers, and sisters, and friends were there. But I was free, and they should be free. I would make a home in the North and bring them there, God helping me. Oh, how I prayed then," she said; "I said to the Lord, 'I'm going to hold steady on to you, and I know you'll see me through.

Tubman awoke one morning in 1862 singing, "My people are free! My people are free!" Later, reflecting on her nineteen dead-of-winter journeys to liberate slaves, she wrote: "I just asked Jesus to take care of me, and He never let me get frost-bitten one bit."

In the twentieth century, progressive social movements called upon god to improve the conditions of the American working class. At the Progressive Political Convention of 1912, the delegates marched down the convention floor singing, "Onward Christian Soldiers." The Reverend George Washington Woodbey, pastor of Mount Zion Baptist Church, ran for Vice President with Socialist Party presidential candidate Eugene Debs. In a powerful dialogue with his Christian mother, Woodbey said he believed that god and the mission of Jesus were compatible with socialism. Eventually, his mother converted to socialism, but never surrendered Jesus. For Woodbey, socialism—the democratization of capital—was the closest political system to the gospel.

The Civil Rights Movement was the last serious invocation of the prophetic god on American soil, as hymns and spirituals became songs of freedom. "I woke up this morning with my mind stayed on Jesus" became "I woke up this morning with my mind stayed on freedom." To the civil rights marchers, Jesus meant both existential and political freedom.

"Somewhere we must come to see that human progress never rolls in on the wheels of inevitability," the Reverend Dr. Martin Luther King, Jr. proclaimed in one of his final sermons. "It comes through the tireless efforts and the persistent work of dedicated individuals who are willing to be co-workers with God." The goal of his Southern Christian Leadership Conference was "to redeem the soul of the nation." King brought into the public space the prophetic African American evangelistic idiom in order to extend the rights of democratic citizenship to his people: "We have waited for more than 340 years for our constitutional and God-given rights," he proclaimed in his famous "Letter from Birmingham Jail." "We will win our freedom because the sacred heritage of our nation and the eternal will of God are embodied in our echoing demands." The relationship between prophetic faith and the covenants of democracy shine most compellingly in his conclusion:

> One day the South will know that when these disinherited children of God sat down at lunch counters, they were in reality standing up for what is best in the American dream and for the most sacred values in our Judeo-Christian heritage, thereby bringing our nation back to those great wells of democracy which were dug deep by the founding fathers in their formulation of the Constitution and the Declaration of Independence.

In what is considered his most "dangerous" speech, "A Time to Break the Silence," King invoked the spirit of Harriet Tubman and Sojourner Truth, declaring that the challenge of calling upon god in the struggle for social justice was a "vocation of agony." Indeed, he gave the speech in the midst of death threats, repudiation from the SCLC's board of directors, and merciless attacks in the mainstream and African-American media.

In the same speech, King also challenged the monopoly on religious discourse shaped by conservative religious individuals and institutions, thereby creating space for the revelation of the prophetic god:

Some of us who have already begun to break the silence of the night have found that the calling to speak is often a vocation of agony, but we must speak. We must speak with all the humility that is appropriate for our limited vision, but we must speak. And, we must rejoice as well, for surely this is the first time in our nation's history that a significant number of its religious leaders have chosen to move beyond the prophesying of smooth patriotism to the high grounds of a firm dissent based upon the mandates of conscience and the reading of history.

King invoked the prophetic god in denouncing "the giant triplets of racism, materialism, and militarism" and criticized the role of the United States in both the manipulation of foreign governments and its treatment of the poor (at home and abroad), which has led to the crisis of democracy we are experiencing today:

A true revolution of values will soon cause us to question the fairness and justice of many of our past and present policies. On the one hand we are called to play the Good Samaritan on life's roadside, but that will be only an initial act. One day we must come to see that the whole Jericho Road must be transformed so that men and women will not be constantly beaten and robbed as they make their journey on life's highway. True compassion is more than flinging a coin to a beggar; it is not haphazard and superficial. It comes to see that an edifice which produces beggars needs restructuring.

This courageous oration transcended the details and consequences of the policies of the U.S. government in order to address the nature of religion and democracy, to show how they are in constant dialogue, and to reveal to us the religious precedents for democratic expansion.

In his last sermon, at Mason Temple Church of God in Christ in Memphis, Tennessee, King linked religion, democracy, and social protest, and demonstrated how they figured into an intimate conversation with striking Memphis sanitation workers:

> We have an injunction and we're going into court tomorrow morning to fight this illegal, unconstitutional injunction. All we say to America is, "Be true to what you said on paper." If I lived in China or even Russia, or any totalitarian country, maybe I could understand the denial of certain basic First Amendment privileges, because they hadn't committed themselves to that over there. But somewhere I read of the freedom of assembly. Somewhere I read of the freedom of speech. Somewhere I read of the freedom of the press. Somewhere I read that the greatness of America is the right to protest for right. And so just as I say, we aren't going to let any injunction turn us around.

King then rhetorically addressed the question of the role of clergy in democracy, which was as tricky a question then as it is now: "Who is it that is supposed to articulate the longings and aspirations of the people more than the preacher?" He acknowledged the presence of clergy from around the country and challenged them to engage in what he called "relevant ministry":

> It's all right to talk about "long white robes over yonder," in all of its symbolism. But ultimately people want some suits and dresses and shoes to wear down here. It's all right to talk about "streets flowing with milk and honey," but God has commanded us to be concerned about the slums down here, and his children who can't eat three square meals a

day. It's all right to talk about the new Jerusalem, but one day, God's preachers must talk about the New York, the new Atlanta, the new Philadelphia, the new Los Angeles, the new Memphis, Tennessee.

This remains the challenge for a contemporary, authentic Religious Left. The levees breached in New Orleans in 2005 exposed a city in which poverty and racism were endemic. These realities coalesced in real-time as the nation watched thousands of its fellow citizens being left to their own devices in the face of a Category Five hurricane. To return New Orleans to its pre-Katrina state, where one-quarter of African-American men and one-third of African-American women lived below the poverty line, would be unjust. My search for meaning during my time in the Lower Ninth Ward led me to ask, as have others: Where was god? Why had not god intervened? How could democracy have failed us so miserably? These questions continue to haunt me even as I find solace in the god of prophesy and hope in the promise and possibility of democracy.

THE FUTURE OF DEMOCRACY IN AMERICA

Martin Luther King's understanding of religion and democracy cut hard against the dominant theology of his time, even within the African American church. In 1958, he and 2,000 other Baptist ministers were expelled from the National Baptist Convention because of their commitment to civil rights. Moreover, of the nearly 500 black churches in Birmingham, Alabama in 1963, only nine participated in the Civil Rights Movement. The "Letter from Birmingham Jail" was partly written in response to local clergymen who found King's presence to be "untimely."

There will be analogous situations today for all of us who enter the prophetic tradition, as there have always been religious forces that have promoted or opposed democratic expansion. The

Bible was used to justify slavery and segregation, but those who participated in the Underground Railroad had a different reading of scripture. Other times, it has been used to justify the status quo, or to do nothing in the face of oppression. We can see this in the experience of the women's movement, and any other movement for democratic expansion. We certainly see it in the contemporary struggle over marriage equality. The reproductive rights movement traces part of its lineage to a United Methodist Women meeting in a church basement in Dallas, Texas. What has moved history and expanded democracy has been prophetic minorities willing to risk life and limb to seize the public's imagination and transform politics and public policy. The thirteenth, fourteenth and fifteenth Amendments to the Constitution, the Civil Rights Act and Voting Rights Act are testament to this tradition.

I believe that an authentic and politically dynamic Religious Left can learn how the reading of scripture in close proximity to the sacred texts of American history and government can offer us a narrative of religious and civic discourse that is centered on the expansion of democratic opportunity. This has long been central to the struggles of African Americans, and is widely accessible and resonant in our culture in the stories of Sojourner Truth, Harriet Tubman, and Martin Luther King. I believe such a narrative can energize and inform a revival of the best of the prophetic tradition and provide a clean break from neo-liberalism and all its variants. This narrative is so powerful, so integral to our nation's history and our highest aspirations as a society, and has played such a profound role in the boldest, most successful movements for social justice, that it can salvage our democracy with an authenticity worthy of the founding of Christianity, and on a scale that could exceed the Protestant reformation.

I realize that this vision will unbelievable to many. But just over hundred and fifty years ago, it would have been inconceivable for me to be writing these words as a free man in my native Arkansas.

PART II.

Memos on Hot Button Issues

A PROGRESSIVE VISION
OF CHURCH-STATE RELATIONS

⇐

REV. BARRY W. LYNN

Some pundits claim that the Religious Right is dead. I'm not joining their chorus. The movement isn't even seriously wounded. Wishing it would go away is like whistling past the graveyard while the zombies are already crawling over the fence.

Similarly, many of the "new evangelicals," although more committed to easing poverty and preserving the environment, still hold to anti-woman, anti-GLBT, anti-constitutional rights agendas. So, what would a genuinely progressive "religious left" do with the Bill of Rights?

No matter where your political ideology takes you, it needs to be rooted in a respect for the Constitution's values. In fact, those are the "values" that define the limits of government power.

I am a progressive Christian minister. I disagree with the way the Religious Right interprets the Bible. I think they get Jesus all wrong. Their theology leaves me cold. I lament the close ties between far-right religions and the federal government that arose during the presidency of Ronald W. Reagan and were cemented under George W. Bush.

That means I want to see a progressive version of Christianity aligned with the government, right? I must want to see our public policies and programs reflect a progressive interpretation of the scriptures, correct?

No way. I have no more interest in a left-wing theocracy than I do a right-wing theocracy. I am anti-theocracy across the board. What I want is a nation that values the rights of all people—religious and non-religious. I want a government that understands that how, if and when you choose to worship is none of its business. I want a government based on secular laws anchored in our secular Constitution. I don't want to see anyone's interpretation of the Bible elevated to public policy.

The Founders made some mistakes. Tolerating slavery and denying women the right to vote were two. But one thing they got right was church-state relations. At a time when just about everyone thought government had to have a religious prop behind it—be it a single state church or some kind of system that favored Christianity generally—our Founders had a bold vision: a secular state backed by a two-pronged guarantee of religious liberty: "Congress shall make no law respecting an establishment of religion, or prohibiting the free exercise thereof...."

To top it off, they included Article VI, which bans religious tests for public office. They gave us a constitution that makes no references to Jesus Christ, Christianity or God. It's a brilliant principle. The Religious Right has spent thirty years trashing it. It say let's abide by it.

What should this mean in practice? This progressive vision of church-state relations rests on a handful of key assumptions:

- *In the eyes of the government, all people are equal and worthy of respect, regardless of what you believe or don't believe about God.* You don't get more rights for having the "correct" faith. You don't get penalized for being an atheist or a non-Christian. Ideally, the government would not even know what you believe or don't believe. It's none of their business.

- *Neutrality, neutrality, neutrality!* All religious groups (and similarly situated secular bodies) are treated equally. A benefit extended to one is extended to all. Burdens are equally shared. No such thing as a "faith-based" initiative exists. The state does not assume a bias toward belief over non-belief. It is not assumed that religious belief is the default standard that makes a "good" American.

- *Government does not co-opt religious symbols and language.* The display of religious symbols and codes is the work of religious bodies. Government does not employ religious rhetoric and borrow its symbols to justify its actions.

- *Theology equals bad public policy.* The government must not adopt theology as the basis for laws that apply to us all. For example, the Religious Right loathes gay people, basing its hate on a few passages from the Bible that it interprets in controversial ways. The government must not deny gays rights based on this reading of the Bible. Holy books, after all, are notoriously open to different interpretations, and some people reject them entirely. The Bible is an important book to many Americans, but that does not mean it was intended to be a manual for governance, any more than it is a science textbook (as assumed by the anti-evolution crowd).

- *Government-backed coercion in religious matters is always unacceptable.* American society is multi-faith and multi-philosophy. It includes people of many different points of view. There is no generic, one-size-fits-all religion suitable for use by government. Mandated prayer has no place in our public schools or government meetings. The decision of how to pray, when to pray or if to pray must always be left to the individual.

- *Science and religion are not enemies.* I believe God endowed us with reason. He intends for us to use it. We need not fear where science will lead us, as long as our exploration is informed by a moral sense that is found in all of the great religious and secular philosophies. (A guiding rule: Seek not to harm others.) Science and medicine must not be forced to bow to the dictates of religious factions. Science and religion are two different ways of understanding the universe. Religion rests on faith; science never can.

- *Federal laws regarding the role of religion in politics must be respected.* Advocates of a progressive view of church and state must be careful not to repeat the mistakes of the Religious Right. Partisan politics has no place in any pulpit. People do not attend worship services to get a list of endorsed candidates. Biased voter guides that attack one candidate and praise another are an abomination. They have no place in our pews. Pastors can discuss issues. They need to refrain from endorsing or opposing candidates from the pulpit or using church resources to help or harm a candidate.

An overriding principle ties together the progressive view on church and state: It is perfectly appropriate, and indeed necessary, for laws to have a secular rationale. This means our nation is legally a secular state. We must not fear this. In fact, we must embrace it. Without the secular state, we are hopelessly at sea.

Why? Secularism, despite what the Religious Right would have you believe, is not a corrosive force. It is not an anti-religious force. Secularism mandates neutrality, not hostility, toward faith. A secular government is one that recognizes that it has no religious functions.

Governments that bulldoze churches, ban private worship and arrest clergy are not promoting secularism. They are promoting hostility toward religion. A secular state allows many religions to flourish. It extends preference toward none but welcomes all. It neither aids nor hinders religion.

America's great religious diversity came about thanks to the secular state. The division of religion and government, as envisioned by leaders like Thomas Jefferson and James Madison as well as religious figures like John Leland and Isaac Backus, led to an explosion of religiosity and helped bring about the Great Awakening. Free from the fear of government punishment, Americans reveled in their liberty. People who were not happy in their churches found or formed others. Self-proclaimed prophets came and went. Some of their churches collapsed, others thrived. Advocates of non-Christian religions didn't fear to come to our shores. Freethinkers challenged all faiths. The secular state sparked a robust exchange of ideas. We are a better nation for this.

Yet even as we've argued, debated and fought over religion, our government, at least in modern times, has been careful not to take sides. And it here that progressives must be cautious. If the pendulum is swinging our way, we must not seek to enlist the government on "our" side of religion.

An example: I believe Jesus expressed a profound and moving concern for the plight of the poor and the sick. The passages in the New Testament where Jesus expresses this view are too numerous to list here. Suffice to say, helping the least among us was a guiding force of Jesus's ministry. So should individual Christians help the poor and sick because Jesus said so? Of course. But a progressive government's rationales must be different. A shared humanity demands that it take into account the plight of those in need.

Imagine a Bible in which Jesus talked about salvation but said nothing about the poor. Would that mean we could ignore them as well? No progressive Christian I know would endorse that view. Many of us are compelled by our faith to help those in need, but we reach out to our brothers and sisters in secular communities and find them equally willing to help. The Bible does not motivate them, yet their vision is no less pristine.

Martin Luther King spoke forcefully of the need to end segregation. He frequently invoked the Bible. As a young man, I was inspired by King's view. It has informed my interpretation of the scriptures in profound ways. Yet there are those who have used the Bible to buttress segregation. They preached from pulpits in the South during the Civil War. To me, they were profoundly and tragically misguided. Still, they pointed to a scripture source.

Rather than have the government say, "This version of scripture is correct, and this one is wrong," I'd prefer the state to say, "Scriptures are irrelevant to the debate. We oppose racial segregation because racial segregation is evil and offensive to the shared values we hold as members of the same species. It will not be tolerated."

It was King himself who consistently called upon people to look to their faith, but the government to look to the Constitution, to do justice. "All we say to America is, 'Be true to what you said on paper,'" King said during a speech at the Mason Temple in Memphis, the night before he was assassinated.

Many progressive Christians are appalled by our failure to adequately protect the environment. I am one of them. I applaud the growing religious movement that seeks to take the threat of global warming seriously. Yet I recognize the limits of an argument that states, "The Bible says God gave us this planet, and thus we have an obligation to care for it." It is too easily countered by someone waving the very same Bible who says, "It doesn't really matter what we do to the planet because Jesus is coming back soon."

Most progressive positions dovetail nicely with secular rationales, thus they can be supported by people of faith and no faith. Contrast this with the policy positions of the Religious Right. What is the secular reason for teaching the Book of Genesis in public school science classes? What is the secular reason for compelling young children to say prayers every day in a public school classroom? What is the secular reason for denying an entire class of Americans—gays and lesbians—basic civil rights? What is the secular reason for erecting a Christian religious symbol in front of city hall?

The leaders of Religious Right organizations have for years argued that all they want is a place at the table, the right to have their voice heard. They've had that for a long time. In fact, their goal is quite different: to own the table and decide who sits there. Too often I've heard those who lead Religious Right groups and those who follow them demand "biblical" government. Conversely, they do not hesitate to label public policy initiatives with which they disagree "unbiblical." Leaders of these groups brag about having a "biblical worldview" and pressure candidates for public office to adopt one as well.

A system of laws based on one faction's interpretation of the Bible is incompatible with democracy. The proper name for governments like that is theocracy. We cannot have a state based on the Bible—either a liberal or a conservative interpretation—simply because our Constitution does not allow it.

Progressives would never use labels such as "unbiblical," recognizing it for what it is: the code language of the theocrats. Yet I cannot help but shudder a bit when I see a progressive politician in a church pulpit on Sunday promise to end homelessness and poverty because Jesus has commanded it. Likewise, I am bothered when I see that same politician accept a political endorsement from a preacher or hold what amounts to a campaign rally in a church.

A question that is rarely posed by the press is simply, "If elected, what role, if any, will your religious beliefs have in determining your domestic or foreign policy?" In my view, the answer should be,

"Even when I have been informed by the ethical teachings of my faith, any implementation of those beliefs must be consistent with the strictures of the Constitution and must be based on more than my ability to cite a text from scripture to justify that position."

More liberal religious voices are needed in these times. They have for too many years been drowned out by the loud, and often coarse, voice of the Religious Right. Yet that progressive voice must be one of inclusion, not exclusion. The Religious Right has made many errors over the years. One of the worst was alienating huge numbers of Americans by telling them that they are little more than second-class citizens who have embraced the "wrong" faith.

Progressives must learn from that mistake. We should welcome a religious voice to the public square, but let us not stop there. Anyone who supports the type of society we want to see—free, open and affirming of all—should be welcomed into our coalition.

I envision not a new progressive religious movement but a new progressive American movement. It will celebrate what is best about our nation, including the genius of our founding document, which guarantees religious and philosophical freedom to all. Religious people will have an important role to play in this movement. Their faith will serve as a source of inspiration, generating the energy and enthusiasm that any true activist movement must have. During church services, they will build alliances and win new support. Their ministers will speak prophetically on behalf of this movement. Yet we will not march under the banner of the cross. Participants will pull their inspiration from many holy books and secular writings, but we'll all be moving forward under the American flag.

This model will avoid the pitfalls of the Religious Right, a movement marked by intolerance, division and often a theology based on hate. As we push forward propelled by a very different vision, one that emphasizes our shared humanity and the civic values that bring us together, we will lift up our voices, some in hymn, others in song, but all in the same key.

Toward a Theology
of Sexual Justice

⇐

REV. DEBRA W. HAFFNER
AND
TIMOTHY PALMER

Many progressive leaders today sense a shift toward moderation among some religious conservatives, as both sides of this seemingly promising trend seek common ground, and a set of shared interests on which a political coalition might be built. But there is a troubling underside: Some well-meaning progressives are privately cautioning advocates for sexual justice to recede quietly into the background.

Their thinking seems to be that abortion and marriage for same-sex couples have polarized the electorate, overshadowing other moral issues. As a result, they argue for a shift in the debate, away from what they dismiss as "pelvic politics" and toward broader concerns, such as poverty and hunger, the war in Iraq and global warming. Their concern is that differences over sexuality will hinder them from forming coalitions with moderate evangelicals and Catholics, thus forestalling the election of progressive candidates. They instead prefer to seek common ground with the right on shared issues.

This approach is narrow-minded and dangerous for millions of people and their families, as abortion and marriage equality cannot be considered peripheral issues by any reasonable standard. Consider that more than a third of American women have had abortions, and that four in 10 Americans have a family member or close friend who is lesbian or gay. Indeed, the full scope of sexual justice embraces anyone who is concerned with gender equality, reproductive rights and health care, and the right to privacy, not to mention education, equality of opportunity and the dignity of all persons. These issues are too important to the well-being of the nation to be buried under "common ground."

SEXUAL JUSTICE IS SOCIAL JUSTICE

The call to sacrifice sexual justice issues is not only wrong, it is counterproductive. Pushing aside women's reproductive rights and equality for lesbian, gay, bisexual and transgender (LGBT) persons would harm the very constituencies that faith communities agree they are most called to serve—people in poverty and children.

Poor women suffer the most when contraception, emergency contraception, and abortion services are not readily available. In the United States, the rate of unintended births is five times greater among poor women than among higher-income women. Between 1994 and 2001, unintended births among poor women actually grew 44 percent. As a result, more than half of the unwanted children in this country are born into poverty. The trends are particularly stark among teenagers. Although teen pregnancy and birth rates have declined by one-third since the early 1990s, one in three American girls still get pregnant by the age of twenty. While rates of sexual activity among lower- and higher-income adolescents are virtually identical, the outcomes are not, as poor and low-income adolescents account for nearly three-quarters of women aged 15-19 who become pregnant.[1]

Consider as well the cost of discrimination for LGBT persons, particularly youth. The 2000 U.S. Census counted nearly 600,000 same-sex households, although the actual number is surely much higher. The American Academy of Pediatrics (AAP) estimates that there are anywhere from 1 to 10 million children living in these homes. Denied the 1,318 marriage benefits currently conferred by federal law, same-sex couples must negotiate an obstacle course to ensure joint-parenting rights, secure family health benefits, and provide the level of stability that married heterosexual couples take for granted. As the AAP concluded, "children of same-gender parents often experience economic, legal and familial insecurity as a result of the absence of legal recognition of their bonds of their non-biological parents." Of course, the burden of legalized discrimination falls heaviest on lower-income families, who cannot afford lawyers to assist them. Similarly, as many as 3 million Americans identify as transgender, many of them still in their teens. Access to affordable health care services specific to their needs is a chronic problem. Therefore, transgender persons who are poor often turn to illegal medications and harmful street procedures because they cannot afford appropriate medical care.[2]

We must not marginalize these issues. We must instead feature them in a broad agenda that supports:

- Comprehensive, age-appropriate sexuality education throughout the life span that includes abstinence, contraception and prevention of sexually transmitted diseases (STDs)

- A responsible approach to adolescent sexuality that recognizes the formation of sexual identity as a key developmental task;

- Full access to affordable, high-quality sexual and reproductive health services, including voluntary contraception, abortion, HIV/STD prevention and treatment, and quality medical services for LGBT persons;

- Full inclusion of women and LGBT persons in religious and public life, including ordination, marriage equality and anti-discrimination laws;

- An understanding and embrace of sexual and gender diversity;

- Support for those who challenge sexual and social oppression and work for justice within their congregations and denominations, and in politics and government;

Progressive religious leaders must adopt a theology of sexual justice. Only then can they enable America's political leaders—not to mention their own congregants—to advance the full social justice agenda that their faith traditions proclaim.

A Theology of Sexual Justice

Sexual justice is not simply a matter of personal piety. Nor it is about what people do in their bedrooms. Rather, the issues go to the heart of what many people of faith believe: that all are created in God's image, and all are called to celebrate the blessings of their sexuality with holiness and integrity.

The Religious Institute on Sexual Morality, Justice, and Healing was founded in 2001 to realize the vision of the *Religious Declaration on Sexual Morality, Justice, and Healing*, a declaration now endorsed by close to 3,000 clergy, theologians and religious educators from more than 45 faith traditions. Since 2001, we have convened colloquia of prominent scholars and clergy from various traditions in order to create a series of open letters that provide a framework for religious leaders to address sexual and reproductive justice in their congregations, and to become advocates in the public square.

The emerging theology of sexual justice focuses on personal

relationships, integrity and justice, rather than on particular sexual acts. All persons have the right and responsibility to lead sexual lives that express love, mutuality, commitment, consent and pleasure. Grounded in respect for the body and for the vulnerability that intimacy brings, this ethic fosters physical, emotional and spiritual health. It accepts no double standards and applies to all persons, without regard to sex, gender, color, age, bodily condition, marital status or sexual orientation.

Children and adolescents. It is in childhood and adolescence that individuals begin to develop the sexual wisdom, values and morality that determine whether they will become sexually healthy adults. Responsible religious leaders want young people to learn about their sexuality not primarily from the media or their peers, but from their parents, faith communities and school-based programs that address the biological, psychological, cultural, ethical and spiritual dimensions of sexuality. These programs must be age-appropriate, accurate and truthful, and have both immediate relevance and applicability for later life.

Young people need help developing their capacity for moral discernment and a freely informed conscience. Education that respects and empowers young people has more integrity than education based on incomplete information, fear and shame. Programs that teach abstinence exclusively and withhold information about pregnancy and sexually transmitted disease prevention fail young people. Children need to know "there is a time to embrace and a time to refrain from embracing," but they also need the skills to make moral and healthy decisions about relationships for themselves, now, and in their adult lives.

Women. A theology of sexual justice compels progressive religious leaders to support a woman's moral agency in all aspects of her life, including her sexual and reproductive health. A woman has the capacity, right and responsibility to make the moral decision as to whether an abortion is justified in her specific circumstances.

That decision is best made when it includes a well-informed conscience, serious reflection, insights from her faith and values, and consultation with a caring partner, family members and spiritual counselor.

Virtually all religious traditions affirm that life is sacred. It is precisely because life and parenthood are precious that no woman should be coerced to carry a pregnancy to term. A theology of sexual justice supports responsible procreation, the widespread availability of contraception, prenatal care and intentional parenting. The sanctity of human life is best upheld when it is not created carelessly.

Religious traditions have different beliefs on the value of fetal life, often according greater value as fetal development progresses. Many traditions affirm that the health and life of the woman must take precedence over the life of the fetus. Scripture neither condemns nor prohibits abortion. It does, however, call people to act compassionately and justly when facing difficult moral decisions. Scriptural commitment to the most marginalized means that pregnancy, childbearing and abortion should be safe for all women. Scriptural commitment to truth-telling means that women must have accurate information as they make their decisions.

A theology of sexual justice respects the right of all people and faiths to set different moral standards. No single religious voice can speak for all faith traditions on abortion, or any other moral issue, nor should government take sides on religious differences. Women must have the right to apply or reject the principles of their faith without legal restriction. Separately, and just as importantly, our constitutional democracy respects the right of individuals to develop their own conscience, religious or otherwise, with government as the guarantor of that right.

Diverse sexualities and genders. Although it is customary to categorize people as male or female, heterosexual or homosexual, this kind of binary thinking fails to reflect the full diversity of human experience. A growing body of social and scientific research about the origins of sexual orientation and gender identity, together with the courageous witness of lesbian, gay, bisexual and transgender people, inspires a theology that affirms sexual and gender diversity as a blessed part of life.

Too many religious institutions have failed to embrace this diversity; worse, many have condemned it. Some have mistakenly called homosexuality sinful when the real issue is heterosexism, or the unjust privileging of heterosexuality. Heterosexism devalues gay, lesbian, bisexual and transgender people just as sexism and male privilege devalue women. Silence, misinformation and condemnation of differing sexual and gender identities create despair, destroy relationships and lead to violence, suicide, even murder. Sexual and gender oppression cannot be portrayed as virtuous and morally defensible.

Biblical references to sexual and gender diversity are relatively rare, and focus primarily on a few verses about male homosexual behavior.[3] The Bible does not address the modern understanding of sexual orientation and gender identity, which contribute to current thinking on human sexuality. Many LGBT people who have been rejected or marginalized by their faith communities find hope in the overarching Biblical call to love and justice.

Progressive religious leaders must help to create a new understanding of sexual and gender diversity, and to promote full equality of LGBT persons in all areas of religious and public life. In denominational terms, this means advocating for welcoming and affirming congregations, ordination of LGBT persons and marriage for same-sex couples. In public policy terms, it means promoting the civil rights of LGBT persons, including anti-discrimination laws, access to health care, adoption rights for LGBT individuals and couples, and marriage equality.

Marriage is an evolving civil and religious institution. In the past, marriage was primarily about property and procreation, whereas today the emphasis is on egalitarian partnership, companionship and love. In the past, neither the state nor most religions recognized divorce and remarriage, interracial marriage or the equality of the marriage partners. These understandings have changed, and rightly so, in the greater recognition of the humanity of all persons and their moral and civil rights. Today, Americans are called to embrace another change, this time the freedom of same-sex couples to marry.

Marriage is about entering into a holy covenant and making a commitment with another person to share life's joys and sorrows. From a social perspective, marriage is valued because it creates stable, committed relationships; provides a means to share economic resources; and nurtures individuals, couples and children. Good marriages benefit the community and express the religious values of long-term commitment, generativity and faithfulness. In terms of these religious and social values, there is no difference in marriage between a man and a woman, two men or two women. Moreover, as many religious traditions affirm, where there is love, the sacred is in our midst.

TRENDS FAVORING SEXUAL JUSTICE

Sexual justice is not only a moral obligation, but a political opportunity, as recent polls clearly show:

- Nearly half of Americans now consider themselves pro-choice, three-quarters favor some level of abortion availability, and most do not want *Roe v. Wade* overturned.[4]

- Similarly, 51 percent of Americans favor either civil unions or full marriage equality for same-sex couples.[5] Even among evangelical Christians, four in 10 support some legal rights for same-sex couples.[6]

- Nearly nine in 10 Americans support federal legislation protecting lesbians and gay men from workplace discrimination,[7] a number that's been rising steadily since the Employment Non-Discrimination Act was introduced in 1996.

- More than eight in 10 Americans favor comprehensive sexuality education in the public schools.[8]

- Support for all of these issues is generally higher among younger Americans than older ones.

This is no time to compromise on sexual justice. Not only is public opinion trending in its favor, but religious and progressive political leaders should not compromise their integrity and their clear obligations. We have an obligation to create a world that embraces the diversity of God's creation and enables all people to live to the fullness of their spirituality and sexuality with holiness and integrity. That is the only common ground where any person of faith should wish to stand.

NOTES

1. *Perspectives on Sexual and Reproductive Health*, January-February 2003.

2. These data are from the authors' *A Time to Seek: Study Guide on Sexual and Gender Diversity*, published in September 2007.

3. The 11 verses that address sexual behavior between men represent .035 percent of the total verses in the Hebrew Bible and New Testament.

4. Gallup poll, 2007.

5. CNN/Opinion Research Corporation poll, 2007.

6. American Values Survey, 2006.

7. Gallup poll, 2007.

8. Sexuality Information and Education Council of the United States (SIECUS)/Advocates for Youth poll, 2000.

REPRODUCTIVE JUSTICE AND A COMPREHENSIVE SOCIAL JUSTICE ETHIC

⇐

REV. DR. CARLTON W. VEAZEY

It is time for the progressive faith community to affirm reproductive justice as inseparable from our overall social justice concerns. Probably the most insidious strategy of the Religious Right has been to use reproductive rights as a wedge issue to divide progressives, and we have not handled this situation as well as we might have. Fortunately, there is a framework that I believe can help us to overcome our divisions and become better, more effective advocates for our values. This model, the reproductive justice framework, is an idea that resonates broadly across our culture and deeply within our faith traditions and offers religious progressives the opportunity to take a fresh look at reproductive issues and incorporate them into a Religious Left agenda.

This is a logical and necessary step in the development of a consistent progressive ethic because reproductive justice underlies and is connected to many of the social justice concerns that progressive religions espouse. In addition, the conditions to achieve reproductive justice are virtually the same as those in other priority areas of interest to the Religious Left: universal health care, the eradication of hunger, eliminating violence, reducing income disparities, improving environmental quality, and increasing security through peace at home and abroad. I believe that including reproductive justice among these concerns will address the issues of many people who are now not receptive to a Religious Left agenda.

The California-based organization Asian Communities for Reproductive Justice, which developed this framework, stipulates that reproductive justice is inherently connected to the struggle for social justice and human rights. There are two main modes of thought that reproductive justice incorporates: "reproductive health" emphasizes the necessary health care services that women need, and "reproductive rights" emphasizes universal legal protections such as *Roe v. Wade*. The reproductive justice framework addresses structural barriers to reproductive health and rights (restrictive laws and lack of access, for example) and envisions the complete physical, mental, and spiritual well-being of all people. It is a broad and compelling concept: it says that reproductive justice will be achieved when all people have the economic, social, and political power and resources to make healthy decisions about their bodies, sexuality, and reproduction.

The prospect of reproductive justice is hopeful—as contrasted with being mired in irresolvable debates about abortion, or singling out what Evelyn Shen of Asian Communities for Reproductive Justice calls "pieces of a woman's body." This framework opens up a deeper discussion that allows us to connect traditional religious concerns such as poverty, violence, hunger, poor healthcare, unequal educational opportunities, and gender and racial/ethnic inequality to reproductive issues. Reproductive justice may be the guiding principle that will allow us, at last, to convey a theological basis, from our respective religious traditions, for public policies that enable women to make reproductive decisions—including abortion decisions—as well as for providing the health, educational and other resources for healthy and wanted pregnancies and strong families.

Here are some sound reasons for the Religious Left to include reproductive justice on its agenda:

- *Connecting the issues makes each stronger:* Keeping the focus limited to abortion and what is termed the unborn child is a barrier to addressing broader justice issues such as poverty alleviation, universal health care, and child development. For example, the growing environmental health movement is raising awareness about the dangers of chemical exposure to male fertility, pregnant women, developing fetuses, and young children. As Sister Joan Chittister writes, a nation that considers itself religious would want to provide "the corporal works of mercy" such as healthcare, housing, food and clean water. "After all, food and education and decent housing and support services are exactly the things that take the strain off families and make abortion unnecessary."

- *Removing barriers to progress:* The intensity around the abortion issue has been a barrier to making progress in expanding access to birth control and family planning, funding comprehensive and medically accurate sex education in public schools, and developing and marketing improved forms of contraception. Consequently, the United States has one of the highest teen pregnancy rates, unintended pregnancy rates and abortion rates among industrialized countries as well as an epidemic of sexually transmitted infections that affects the ability to have children and increases the risk of serious diseases such as cervical cancer.

- *Increasing understanding of "values":* The misperception of the 2004 election that abortion was a chief concern of "values voters" has had negative consequences for women's health issues. Too many politicians took this fallacious interpretation of the vote as permission to retreat from safeguarding legal abortion and supporting measures to protect women's health. Several ill-conceived legislative proposals were introduced that focused narrowly on abortion reduction without seriously addressing the prevention of unintended pregnancy. An empowered Religious Left would expose such political pandering around the issue of abortion and reinforce that the "values" of great importance to most Americans include economic equality, peace, and a clean environment, and that these are all intimately connected to reproductive health.

- *Building political support:* Political leaders may increase their support for prevention when religious constituencies speak out in favor of such programs as family planning, health services, and sex education and relate them to concerns such as poverty alleviation and child health.

- *Reinforcing the meaning of religious freedom:* The opposition to comprehensive sex education, HIV/AIDS prevention that includes condom education, emergency contraception and legal abortion comes from religious groups that claim these violate religious beliefs—the underlying message being that the only valid religious beliefs are theirs. The failure to appreciate and articulate religious pluralism as a powerful value often leads to capitulation and compromise on reproductive issues with factions that do not honor the differing value systems inherent in our religiously plural society, as well as the value of religious pluralism itself.

A Religious Left that is unwaveringly committed to protecting religious freedom and enabling religious pluralism to flourish should speak with one voice against all attempts to violate church/state separation, including in areas of reproductive decision-making.

Even as we work to embrace reproductive justice as a logical expression of our religious values, having a serious dialogue in religious and political circles on reproductive justice will be challenging. The issue of abortion has created fear and division among progressives and hampered our efforts to forge a broad movement for justice that includes both women's rights and religious organizations. So-called "renewal groups" that use the abortion issue to create divisiveness in mainline Protestant denominations and Catholic and evangelical groups that oppose abortion can be expected to resist efforts to broaden the discussion to connect to other social justice issues. But research shows that the public is tired of the seemingly unending divisiveness on abortion and would like positive programs to support healthy and wanted pregnancies, keep young people in school, expand healthcare, and strengthen families. With that in mind, the Religious Left should move ahead to incorporate reproductive justice in a comprehensive ethic of social justice.

CREATING THE CONDITIONS FOR STRONG FAMILIES AND WANTED CHILDREN

Religions including The United Methodist Church, the Presbyterian Church (USA), The Episcopal Church, the United Church of Christ, Unitarian Universalism and all branches of Judaism agree that human life is sacred—and include the life of the woman as well as the potential child. It is because of this belief that many religious communities work for a world in which every child is wanted, loved and cared for, which is why they support birth control, family planning, safe and legal abortion, and health care for all.

The reality, though, is that 82 percent of the approximately 750,000 teen pregnancies in the United States each year are unintended, with lifelong consequences for the teen mothers and their families. According to the National Campaign to Prevent Teen and Unplanned Pregnancy, teen pregnancy is closely linked to a host of other critical social issues, including poverty and income disparities, overall child well-being, out-of-wedlock births, responsible fatherhood, health issues, education, child welfare, and risky behaviors. In addition, there are more than 500,000 births a year from pregnancies that women themselves say they did not want at the time of conception, or in the months preceding the birth. These children are particularly vulnerable. For example, even when taking into account various social and economic factors, women experiencing an unplanned pregnancy are less likely to obtain prenatal care, making their babies at increased risk of being born prematurely and at a low birth weight. These babies are also less likely to be breastfed, and are more likely to face a range of developmental risks such as poor physical and mental health compared to children born as the result of an intended pregnancy.

CREATING THE CONDITIONS FOR RESPONSIBLE PARENTING

While an enduring commitment to family relationships is a bedrock religious value, many current social policies have the effect of weakening families because of a lack of regard for reproductive justice. Again, unintended and unwanted pregnancies put women and families at risk for numerous problems that are intertwined with many of the social justice concerns that progressive religions espouse. Most unplanned births occur to unmarried women, and these families are more likely to be poor and the children are more likely to drop out of high school, have lower grade-point averages, lower college aspirations, and poor school attendance records. "If more children in this country were born to parents who are ready and able to care for them," says the National Campaign to Prevent Teen and Unplanned Pregnancy, "we would see a significant reduction in a host of social problems afflicting children in the United States, from school failure and crime to child abuse and neglect."

CREATING A HEALTH CARE SYSTEM THAT WORKS FOR ALL

The call for universal health care is coming from churches, temples, synagogues and seminaries. Reproductive healthcare is integral to any reasonable definition of health care, yet new data indicates that there are problems in terms of access to health care services. One consequence, according to the federal Centers for Disease Control and Prevention, is that maternal mortality in the United States has been rising—as of 2004, it was at its highest rates since the 1970s. In addition, the maternal mortality rate among African American women is at least three times higher than among white women, an indicator of racial disparities in health services. Three studies have shown that at least 40 percent of maternal deaths could have been prevented with improved quality of care. If we are serious about universal health care, we must advocate for the health and well being of the whole person, including women's reproductive health care.

CREATING A MORE JUST WORLD

While most religions understands that the scriptural injunction to love your neighbor and care for "every living thing that moves on the earth" applies across national boundaries, 500,000 women die each year in impoverished and developing countries from pregnancy-related causes, including unsafe and illegal abortions, pregnancies at very young ages that cause irreparable physical damage, and pregnancies that occur too frequently. In addition, 9.7 million children die before they turn five years of age—including nearly 40 percent in the first month of life. It is estimated that more than 6 million maternal, newborn and child deaths would be averted yearly if essential maternal, newborn and child health and nutrition interventions were implemented at scale.

Throughout the world, women's struggle for dignity includes the ability to consent to sex, to have a decision in childbearing, and to be able to care for themselves and their families. Healthy families are key to economic progress. These are values that are integral to an agenda for peace and sustainable global environmental practices.

CONCLUSION

The current and prospective Religious Left faces a significant challenge in how and even, for some, whether to address reproductive justice. The options are clear. We can continue to give lip-service to the issues of reproductive justice, rejecting theses issues as too divisive. Or we can directly address them because they are of the most profound concern to women and men throughout the world. If we choose the latter, as I believe we must, our central challenge is to show how reproductive justice is deeply rooted in our religious values and to do so in ways that are affirming and respectful of diverse religious views. For us to do anything less is to risk failing as healers of humanity and prophets of a comprehensive vision of a just world.

Marjorie Brahms Signer of the Religious Coalition for Reproductive Choice provided research and editorial assistance in the development of this essay.

CREATIONISM, EVOLUTION AND THE INTEGRITY OF SCIENCE AND RELIGION

⇐

DR. PETER M. J. HESS

The casual observer of American public life might be excused for concluding that the armies of science are locked in mortal combat with the armies of religion. That is largely because there are many who are heavily invested in the so-called "warfare thesis" that portrays Christianity (and especially the Catholic Church) as having doggedly stood in the way of scientific progress for centuries. This thesis is, however, based on profoundly mistaken assumptions.

As a theologian, I work with both scientists and members of religious communities to show that there is no inherent conflict between faith and reason; between and religion and science. My position at the National Center for Science Education in Oakland, California focuses on issues related to evolution and religion. I especially enjoy working with Christians who unwittingly regard "evolution or creation" as a dichotomy, and who are attracted to Intelligent Design Creationism or Young Earth Creationism. Most are unaware that there is a sound alternative that is respectful of scientific principles and faithful to traditional religious practice and belief in God. It is called "theistic evolution."

I'd like to offer a few points for a prospective Religious Left to consider as it approaches these matters in politics and public policy.

Before proceeding, however, we should acknowledge that there exists a very real culture war, characterized by skirmishes both within and between churches, political parties, and academic and civic institutions. Let's take a quick look at a few recent flash points.

The creationist organization "Answers in Genesis" opened a museum in 2007 in northern Kentucky complete with elaborate dioramas demonstrating that humans peacefully coexisted with vegetarian *Tyrannosaurus rexes*, and even saddled and rode some dinosaurs a few thousand years ago. A 2008 film, *Expelled: No Intelligence Allowed*, claims that "intelligent design" has been unjustly expelled from academe; alleges that the theory of evolution leads to atheism; and charges that Darwinism provided the moral justification for Hitler's Nazi concentration camps.

In sharp reaction to such attacks on science, a number of authors representing the so-called "new atheism"—including Sam Harris and Richard Dawkins—have mounted a vigorous assault not only on the various forms of scientific creationism, but on religious belief itself.

As "evolutionists" and "creationists" parry and thrust in pulpit and classroom, in print and in courthouse, a number of questions demand attention. Are the practices of religion and science in some fundamental way opposed? Must scientific and religious interpretations of reality be regarded as mutually exclusive? Since our religiously plural society is unambiguously established upon the separation of church and state, how can we resolve the perennial disputes about how science and religion should be addressed in public schools?

AN EPISTEMOLOGICAL HOUSE CLEANING

Any prospective Religious Left that seeks to protect the integrity of both science and religion will need to begin with a good epistemological house-cleaning. Properly speaking, science and religion occupy different spheres of knowledge. Science asks "how" questions: What is it? How does it happen? By what processes? Meanwhile, religion asks "why" questions: What is life's meaning? What is my purpose? Is the world of value? These are complementary rather than conflicting perspectives. Einstein's somewhat overstated epigram is helpful in highlighting how this is so: "Science without religion is lame, religion without science is blind." Each should respect the autonomy of the other, and when they don't, trouble is afoot.

I am often asked, "Do you believe in creation or in evolution?" Framed this way, I am forced to choose between an apparently atheistic evolutionary worldview and scientifically naïve creationism. I often respond that this question rests upon a category mistake and sets up a false opposition. To illustrate this I hold up an orange and ask my students, "is this fruit orange or spherical?" Usually at least one student will recognize that "orange" and "spherical" are not contradictory but complementary descriptions of the fruit.

I then ask them whether the disjunctive question "do you believe in creation or evolution?" is meaningful. As in the case of the orange, "creation" and "evolution" are not in competing categories, but rather are complementary ways of looking at the universe. To oppose them is to commit a category mistake. "Creation" is in the category of a metaphysical concept; it is the philosophical belief that the universe is not self-subsistent, but that it depends for its existence upon something or some being outside itself. An empirically untestable belief in its most general form, "creation" makes no claims about how or when the world came to be, or even whether creation was an "act" or an event. It is a philosophical tenet compatible with the theological doctrines of Judaism, Christianity, Islam, and other monotheistic religions. A contrary (and equally untestable) metaphysical assertion would be that the universe is uncreated, or self-subsistent.

By contrast, "evolution" is in a scientific category—a biological theory that all life is related through descent with modification from common ancestors. It is physical, not metaphysical. Like gravitation, atomic structure, plate tectonics and other theories, evolution makes no claims about God's existence or non-existence, and in fact is compatible with theism, atheism, and agnosticism.

The Religious Right, however, generally differs with just about everyone else over the definitions of science and religion. Science may be defined as "a process of explaining phenomena by testing explanations against the natural world," with the important element being testing, rather than the simple acceptance of an explanation based on authority or personal preference. This is followed by operation within the framework of methodological naturalism. But the Religious Right generally asserts that science does not merely limit itself to natural causes in its methodology, but that it promotes the idea that "God had nothing to do with it," in order to develop and push a purely naturalist philosophy. As a result, they fear that an all-encompassing atheistic worldview antithetical to every value they hold dear is being foisted upon the public.

The Religious Right and the culture of the Left have as divergent understandings of religion as they do of science. Religion may be reasonably defined as "a system of beliefs and practices directed to interpreting and responding to the perceived sacred dimension of the universe." This fairly describes both theistic and non-theistic religious systems, tested as they are by their coherence and their responsiveness to the lived experience of the believing community. For the Religious Right, however, religion is usually understood to be the cornerstone of American society and its freedoms, the foundation of societal values, and the final arbiter of truth. For Christian fundamentalists, this usually also requires accepting Biblical inerrancy, a hermeneutical principle even more foundational than a literalist reading of scripture, and with as weighty implications for science.

Although the religious and political Left is far more varied in the range of its positions, most embrace traditional approaches to freedom of religious expression and separation of church and state. But some have, unfortunately, adopted the fervent anti-religion-ism of the "new atheism," as epitomized by Richard Dawkins. "The universe we observe," he wrote in *River Out of Eden: A Darwinian View of Life* (1995), "has precisely the properties we should expect if there is, at bottom, no design, no purpose, no evil and no good, nothing but blind pitiless indifference." Such views have led many to see Dawkins and other scientists who write about religion as having stepped outside the bounds of legitimate methodological naturalism into a metaphysical naturalist creed that represents not science, but scientism. In so doing, they become as much a carica-ture of "science" as the Religious Right is a caricature of "religion."

CREATIONISM, INTELLIGENT DESIGN AND THE WAR ON SCIENCE

Historically, creationists have employed three main strategies in their fight against evolution since the 1925 Scopes trial. One is to claim—with no scientific foundation_that evolution is a "theory in crisis," proclaiming that evolution is "theory, not fact." This claim confuses the everyday definition of "theory" as "guess" with the well-established definition that a scientific theory is a well-tested, systematic explanation of observed facts. The theory of evolution is among the most important, well-tested theories in all of science; and yet it is singled out for attack with this slogan.

A second tactic has been to represent evolution and religion as mutually contradictory, despite the fact that most mainline churches and countless theologians have assimilated the evolution-ary perspective into their theologies (see http://www.issr.org.uk/id-statement.asp). Yet a third approach has been to push for equal time for creationist and evolutionary ideas in science classrooms. "Creation science" is a political movement based on the idea that a biblical literalist view of creation is supported by science. "Creation" is the ancient and theologically appropriate doctrine that the world is dependent for its being on God, believed by Christians, Muslims and religiously observant Jews. The term was hijacked by Protestant Fundamentalists early in the twentieth century and has come to be applied almost exclusively to a worldview characterized by a scientifically naïve belief in a geologically young Earth and a global Noachian Flood.

When the Supreme Court ruled in 1987 (*Edwards v. Aguillard*) that "creation science" is religion rather than science, the movement adapted. Creation science continues to be strong in some segments of the culture, but one branch, led by the Seattle-based Discovery Institute since the 1990s, evolved into the "Intelligent Design" movement. Intelligent Design (ID) advocates falsely portray evolution as being challenged in the world of science, and seek to insert ID into public school curricula under the slogan "teach the controversy." Although there are lively debates about the details of evolution, there is no controversy among biologists about the validity of the theory itself. In 2005 a federal judge declared that the Dover, Pennsylvania school district's policy of teaching ID was unconstitutional because it "is not science and cannot be judged a valid, accepted scientific theory as it has failed to publish in peer-reviewed journals, engage in research and testing, and gain acceptance in the scientific community." The most recent threat from ID is making an end run around the Dover decision by encouraging science teachers to teach the "strengths and weaknesses" of evolution.

HOW SHOULD WE ENGAGE THE RELIGIOUS RIGHT?

The National Center for Science Education is a national clearing house for information about evolution and creationism, textbook and science standards policy, and creationist strategies (www.ncseweb.org/). When engaging the Religious Right on evolution and creationism our extensive experience suggests:

1. Begin by defending the integrity of both science and religion, and their autonomy to operate within their own respective spheres of competence.

   (a) Science can only operate within a framework of methodological naturalism. When it introduces super-naturalistic principles (such as an intelligent designer) into the explanation, it ceases to be science. Likewise, when a person in a position of scientific authority proclaims that science logically leads to metaphysical naturalism, atheism, or theism, he or she has stepped outside the bounds of science. Scientists when speaking as scientists should not proclaim that science compels any metaphysical position.

   (b) Religion and theology similarly are constrained to remain within their sphere of competence, which is to practice, lead, profess, exhort about, and expound upon the spiritual dimension of human life. In their professional capacity, religious professionals may legitimately weigh in on ethical issues raised by science, such as stem cell research and cloning. But theologians and religious leaders are in no position to dictate the terms of scientific methodology.

2. Reinforce that the United States was established upon the principle of the separation of church and state; thus sectarian views like Creationism should not be advocated in the classroom.

3. Make it clear that the content of science classes should reflect the consensus view of science as determined by scientists, not politicians.

4. Advocate exposure to the diverse religious traditions that comprise our pluralistic culture, as part of basic cultural literacy. The legitimate place in public education for teaching about creation stories is social studies classes, where stories will be described but never advocated, nor offered as an alternate scientific theory.

In short, a coherent Religious Left approach to the teaching of science and religion in the public schools will be greatly assisted by a clear understanding of the controversy between evolution and its various creationist opponents.

The author is grateful to Eugenie Scott and Glenn Branch of the National Center for Science Education for judiciously critiquing the final draft of this essay.

TAKE IT FROM A
STEM CELL CATHOLIC

⇐

FRANK COCOZZELLI

Getting the issue of stem cell research right is vital for any prospective Religious Left. The good news, however, is that there are ways to navigate this tricky issue through the concerns of those across the religious and political spectrum.

Most people—left, right and center—are concerned about the ethics of inventing and patenting life, but also want medical science to use every means to try and cure serious and debilitating health problems. Reflecting these conflicting attitudes, most religious institutions are not of a single mind when it comes to the issue of stem cell research. Some are in favor of all or most forms of stem cell research while others, especially my own Catholic Church, are opposed. Organizing members of various religious traditions into a coherent Religious Left in which stem cell research is part of, and not peripheral to the agenda is a key to not only advancing this promising avenue of research, but also making treatments broadly accessible, unleashing hope for those who are afflicted by conditions that could benefit from stem cell generated treatments, such as myself.

January 21, 2008 was a good day from me. That day, researchers at the University of Texas Southwestern made a significant break-through in the treatment of muscular dystrophy. Using genetic manipulation techniques in mice, they were able to transform embryonic stem cells into muscle cells. Most importantly, they were able to do so without the appearance of tumors, a problem that plagues stem cell research.

Why was this good news for me? Because I have a form of LMG muscular dystrophy. When I was first diagnosed in 1985, I walked with a slight limp. Today, my condition has deteriorated to the point where I am bound to a wheelchair, a virtual quadriplegic. Yet this disability has not kept me from living my life and continuing my work as an attorney, and, for the last seven years, fighting an uphill battle for federal funding and oversight for embryonic stem cell research.

It was through the window of research into my illness that I first learned about the threats to religious pluralism and to liberal democracy from a small group of "intellectuals" commonly known as neoconservatives, and their religious allies. The political power of this alliance quickly became apparent after I received the real first bit of hopeful news on my condition from the world of medical science.

One morning during the summer of 2000, while my wife was getting me dressed for court, we heard a report on the *Today Show* that President Bill Clinton was going to allow for the federal funding of embryonic stem cell research. In December 1998, my neurologist had told us of this then-recent discovery and how it offered so much hope not just for me, but for countless others suffering from different diseases and disabilities. He told us that the research was not a guarantee, but at least offered real hope for possible treatment.

However, this hope was dashed by the neoconservative-influenced presidency of George W. Bush.

KNOWING THE OPPOSITION; DEFENDING OUR FRIENDS

Since that day in 2000, I have come to realize that the principal opposition to stem cell research, in addition to the aforementioned neoconservative movement, comes from prominent Protestant fundamentalists of the Religious Right, and, in the Catholic Church, from members of a secretive rightist group called group called Opus Dei, and leading neoconservatives. These elements see embryonic stem cell research as a symptom of liberal democracy and its progeny—modernity. To increase their power, the activities of these groups are often coordinated through think tanks such as the Institute on Religion and Democracy (IRD) and the Ethics and Public Policy Center. This has been especially significant, as the IRD, whose leadership comprises all three of these groups, has, for the last quarter century, waged a well-financed campaign to disrupt, divide and destabilize the mainline Protestant denominations, some of which are strong supporters of embryonic stem cell research. This campaign has had the effect of turning the churches inward, increasing congregational in-fighting, which renders them less able to advance their progressive social witness in the world.

What has helped me enormously, and I suggest would help to inform and empower a more politically dynamic and vastly more effective Religious Left approach to the matter of embryonic stem cell research, is learning more about the nature of our most formidable opponents. After all, how can we craft a successful political strategy without a healthy knowledge of the opposition—especially the religious opposition to some of the most hopeful medical research in modern times?

THE NEOCONS

Originally inspired by the teachings of philosopher Leo Strauss, many (though, not all) neoconservatives subscribe to the belief that the ancient Greek philosopher Plato had developed the perfect pattern for an orderly society. In Plato's view, while Democracy was acceptable, it was only meant for social elites, as was the case in ancient Athens. In this model, everyone had their station in life, and should accept it. Science was for the advancement of knowledge, not for the ability to harness its own lessons in order to overcome nature's hardships such as disease and disability. Suffering, whether from war or from illness, was what produced true heroism.

Religious orthodoxy plays a central role in modern neoconservative thought. For many of the movement's disciples, it is the glue that holds society together. And for that reason, religious dissent is frowned upon. This dovetails nicely with the similar neo-Platonist view of many ultra-orthodox Catholics, one defined by the twelfth-century theologian Bernard of Clairvaux's statement that "faith is to be believed, not disputed." Rational inquiry is not for the masses, but for an elite philosopher class.

The practitioners of neo-conservatism, whether Christian, Jewish and indeed, even atheist, are always on the offensive: condemning dissenters of good will, inveighing against sound science and preaching a generic but wrathful orthodoxy that is exclusionary to the point of bitterness. It is all an attempt to impose a new American morality via the power of corporate wealth to control the social policies of mainstream Christian denominations while essentially neutralizing the more progressive, but ancient teachings of Judaism. Their ultimate goal is a theocracy of sorts, based upon a conglomeration of traditionalist-but-wrathful Christian orthodoxies channeled to serve a foreign policy based upon American hegemony in conjunction with *laissez-faire* economics.

Many neoconservatives argue that the framers of the Constitution erred by agreeing to the Establishment Clause of the First Amendment. Irving Kristol is at the forefront of this Strauss-inspired argument. Like Strauss, Kristol believes that a strict, orthodox religion is vital to national cohesion. Not only is the "myth" of religious belief necessary to maintain societal order, but the "myth" to be imposed must be one that calls for a vengeful, furious deity that inspires fear in the governed.

The greater issue, however, is modernity. Both Straussian-inspired neoconservatives as well as ultra-orthodox Catholics rail against the supposed abandonment of neo-platonic, classical values in contemporary America. Embryonic stem cell research clearly interferes with this scenario because it demystifies science and, in their eyes, removes the virtue of human heroism. Such views have been ascendant in the Vatican since the installation of the neo-Platonist minded Pope John Paul II.

However, reexamination of church doctrines in light of urgent modern needs and the advances of science are not, as the neo-Platonists and the neo-cons would have it, a form of apostasy. Instead, it is the quest to strengthen faith through reevaluation while we strive to make a better world for the people of God. Indeed, Jesus' healing of the sick and disabled was in accordance with the halakic notion of Pikuach nefesh—the admonition to save lives in being. There is a very similar concept in Christian thought known as Epikiea. Great thinkers of the Judeo-Christian tradition have always understood that doctrine can be a form of idolatry, such that we lose sight of the greater good. And seeing this is the nature of the change we now need to do the greatest good.

FIGHTING BACK

To counter the threats to liberal Democracy and enlightened Catholicism from neoconservatives and their allies such as Opus Dei, in 2006 I joined up with like-minded religious progressives to found an ecumenical think tank, the Institute for Progressive Christianity. I began also to blog regularly at the web sites *Talk to Action* (www.talk2action.org) and *Cross Left* (www.crossleft.org) about stem cell research and the broader dangers from neo-conservatism and the

Religious Right. All of these activities have helped me clarify my own thinking and to network with religious and non-religious progressives.

Together, our hope is that a Religious Left, embracing deeply held and broad moral principles, will seek to advance a common politics, one that is guided by moral outcomes and moral means of getting there, informed by advances in science and medicine, and adapted to our moment in history. A Religious Left serious about these things will also seek to understand the strengths and weaknesses of its formidable opponents, incorporating this knowledge into an evolving strategy, valuing our friends and coming to their aid when they are under attack. A strengthened Religious Left would defend these institutions against such attacks inside the churches, as well as outside in the public square.

Are We More Devoted to Order or to Justice?

⇐

KETY ESQUIVEL

What would a politically dynamic Religious Left approach to immigration look like, assuming an active, interfaith political movement? I think in answer to that, we face a few profound, but simple choices: Will we choose to be fearful, greedy nativists or loving, patriotic people of faith? Will we be effective in our quest for justice, or will we fail to learn from history? Will we devote ourselves more to the established order, or to justice?

I believe that the unprecedented immigration marches of 2006 can help us imagine what is possible and who we can choose to be. In the spring of 2006, religious and political organizations came together to defend the alien in this country. Over the course of four months, in more than one hundred cities across the country, millions of people gathered in the streets in opposition to unjust nativist legislation. In some cities, the protestors numbered more than a half million.

We must remember our history, for our present is informed by all that came before. In 1492, Columbus brought Europeans to "the New World" and after him came successive waves of immigrants to a land already inhabited by an indigenous people. Some of these immigrants came voluntarily, some involuntarily. During each successive wave, many were met with prejudice and bigotry, and treated as aliens and/or outsiders.

A Letter to Us from Birmingham Jail

The history of African Americans is different than most of the other streams of immigration. To date, we are still striving to fulfill the prophetic dream of Martin Luther King Jr., but his words about the struggle speak through time in ways that can inform our current circumstances. "I must make two honest confessions to you, My Christian and Jewish brothers," King famously wrote in his "Letter from Birmingham Jail." "First, I must confess that over the past two years I have been gravely disappointed with the white moderate. I have almost reached the regrettable conclusion that the Negro's great stumbling block in his stride toward freedom is not the White Citizen's Councilor or the Ku Klux Klanner, but the white moderate, who is more devoted to 'order' than to justice; who prefers a negative peace which is the absence of tension to a positive peace which is the presence of justice; who constantly says: 'I agree with you in the goal you seek, but I cannot agree with your methods of direct action'; who paternalistically believes he can set the timetable for another man's freedom; who lives by a mythical concept of time and who constantly advises the Negro to wait for a 'more convenient season.'

Shallow understanding from people of good will is more frustrating than absolute misunderstanding from people of ill will. I had hoped that the white moderate would understand that law and order exist for the purpose of establishing justice and that when they fail in this purpose they become dangerously structured dams that block the flow of social progress."

The obstacles that King identified are similar to what we face today with regard to immigration. Do the current laws exist for the purpose of establishing justice, or are they dams blocking the flow of social progress? Are our moderate sisters and brothers in the pews more devoted to order or to justice? Will they be joining their immigrant brothers and sisters in the street demanding change? Will they be calling their representatives, voting or running for office with a prophetic vision of justice for the alien in their hearts and minds?

Those with the most power to do justice are often reluctant to experience the discomfort of seriously addressing social change. We are divided by the usual obstacles of demographics and geography, as well as the exclusivity and reductionism of single issue politics. This is true in part because particular injustices are necessarily rooted in and supported by wider, systemic injustices that can be hard to understand and more than a little daunting when it comes to thinking about how to address them. We all know this, but getting underneath the immediacy of the issue to the systemic issues can be troubling.

We have a long history of migration of labor and exploitation across the American border that is too easy to forget. The plan which brought massive numbers of Chinese to build the railroads in the nineteenth century was based on nativism and greed. The bracero program of 1942, which survived in one form or another until the 1960s, was accused of egregious human rights abuses. Any proposal that creates a two-tiered nation of citizens and immigrant hired hands free to work forever as guest workers, but never allowed to join our nation as citizens must be whole-heartedly rejected by a Religious Left.

As people of faith we have a clear mandate to love and welcome the alien. Our scripture couldn't be clearer. In Leviticus 19:34, we are told that "the alien who resides with you shall be to you as a citizen among you." Deuteronomy 10:19 tells us to "love the stranger, for you yourselves were once strangers." In Exodus 22:21, it states that we can not "wrong or oppress a resident alien" because we "know the heart of an alien" since we were once aliens

ourselves. And Jesus warns us in Mathew 25:43, "I was a stranger....
and you did not welcome me..."

We must realize that scapegoating immigrants helps us to
avoid addressing economic issues that run wide and deep. We can
and must oppose the hatred, but we must dig further to address
the systemic issues as well.

Recent trade agreements are a source of much of the problem.
I can tell you from personal observation that NAFTA has caused
economic devastation in the home nation of many émigrés. There
are cities in Latin America which lack a significant male population, as the men have had to wander north to find work in order
to feed their families because back home, there are no longer any
jobs, in part because the jobs that had left the U.S. soon fled Latin
America to go to China.

The exploitation of workers at home and abroad in order to
have the cheapest products possible is a game which by design,
we will lose. There are always poorer, more desperate people who
will work for less and countries that will do little to protect the
environment and workers rights. As people of faith, we need to be
able to confront our desire to enjoy an abundance of inexpensive
products while turning a blind eye to outrageous exploitation.

We must also know our history and take pride in the pivotal
role of those who came before us in the struggle, such as the aboli-
tionists, the Labor movement, the Civil Rights Movement and the
Sanctuary Movement, to name a few. Inevitably, we will witness
and encounter many of the same obstacles that King describes in
his letter. In spite of that, we must press on.

OVERCOMING OBSTACLES TO JUSTICE IN OUR TIME

Believing that the solution could be found in politics and government, in 2003 I left an international corporate job and joined
a presidential campaign. I was inspired by my candidate and the

exciting promise of what can come from electoral victory. However, I soon saw that the way campaigns are currently run leads to "politics as usual." The positioning on issues becomes opportunistic and a litmus test is applied to determine what might garner the most votes. Positions are only rarely based on principle, and I soon found that there was little that I (and maybe anyone) could do to change this within the campaign system itself.

In response to this realization, I was drawn to the open sourcing of politics on the Internet and together with a friend in 2005, I created Cross Left (www.crossleft.org.) Soon after that came a grassroots think tank, The Institute for Progressive Christianity. As a Christian I recognized that the Religious Right was not going to do or say anything to correct the injustices I saw, and therefore they did not in any way represent the people of faith that I knew. So we created our own platforms for us to be able to speak from our own values as Christians.

But as I engaged in the struggle, I came to a deeper understanding of King's Letter, and the kinds of resistances we encounter in the face of prophetic social change. I remember conversations with activists in San Francisco who were shocked by the massive immigrant led, pro-immigrant marches in 2006. Participants in the marches in the cities were, for the most part, people of color, youth and people of faith; and I remember being dumbfounded that with the exception of front page articles, the message did not go out into the suburbs nor did it permeate the progressive movement, which was focused on the war on Iraq. I remember telling my progressive friends that it was critical that we not see this pro-immigrant movement as being in competition with the anti-war movement, but rather as a compliment to it.

Taken together, these parallel movements suggested to me a re-imagining of what this great nation could be. If only, I thought, we could harness the energy of both movements: the pro-immigrant movement being mostly working people of color and their children, and the anti-war movement being mostly well-educated and white. I also remember thinking that there was a great opportunity for the message of these struggles to be brought into the pulpits of suburban places of worship so that we could unite on this matter of justice. But that was not to be. When these remarkable marches—the most visible marches for justice since the Civil Rights Movement—were over, normalcy returned, and they were soon forgotten.

Now I find myself taking satisfaction in some victories, even as we have a long way to go. The Catholic Bishops have called for comprehensive immigration reform and the Methodist Affirmation is an inspiring one. And yet, we still have so far to go. For many in the pews, the topic of the undocumented still brings fear of the other, rather than the parable of the Good Samaritan to mind. Yet as a Religious Left, we seem to be nearly as atomized as ever; divided between issue priorities, as well as by race and class and certainly the lack of a wider sense of movement and an operational strategy.

But as in movements which came before us, I think it is time for us, as a Religious Left, to begin raising our voices in inspiration. We have the voice of God within us, the light. Let it shine. Let us show those who think that it is easiest to scare people and therefore control them that we stand with our eyes wide open, creating our own destiny and calling for there to be heaven on earth, love, freedom and hospitality.

Regarding immigration, Archbishop of San Antonio José Gómez has stated: "We are Catholics and Americans. We should never be forced to choose between these two identities. We must live every day in this culture as men and women of faith." I believe his words ring true for all people of faith. We must live as people of faith and good Americans, our faith informing our values, which in turn govern our politics. I contend a Religious Left has to approach the politics of immigration from the values of love and hospitality. We need to be prepared to call out those who are motivated by fear, greed and pride.

Let us therefore, make immigration an integral part of a political agenda of a unified, politically dynamic Religious Left. Let us also allow our understanding of the many aspects of immigration to illuminate our understanding of the economy, and much more. Things pass from vogue, but we can not allow that to happen here. Let us hold ourselves, our elected representatives, and all parts of society to account, demanding *palabras y hechos*—words and actions—which support our vision of a just nation on the issue of immigration.

PART III.

Getting from Here to There

Wrong About the Right

⇐

DR. JEAN HARDISTY
AND
DEEPAK BHARGAVA

Editor's note: Although some elements of this article may feel a bit dated, having originally appeared in the November 7, 2005 edition of the Nation, its main points remain as timely now as when they were written.

The now dominant narrative about the right's rise to power holds that conservatives invested huge amounts of money in a number of think tanks over the past thirty years and brilliantly framed their messages in ways that were simple and resonated deeply with much of the American public. By embracing a top-down, hierarchical movement structure and relentless message discipline, the right was able not only to triumph at the ballot box but also to change the very terms of political discussion—demonizing "big government" and celebrating "tax relief," "personal responsibility" and "free-market capitalism." This account of conservative strategy has piqued the interest of a growing number of progressive groups, who argue that the left should adopt a similar strategy. And it is currently driving the activities of many major progressive donors.

The difficulty here is that, as an explanation of the right's ascendancy, it is at best incomplete and at worst misleading. What's more, it is not clear that progressives should emulate all of the right's tactics, or that we will succeed by doing so. There are certainly lessons to be learned from the right—but for the most part they are different from those commonly assumed. Here is an alternative view of the insights progressives should take away from three decades of conservative domination.

SECRETS OF THEIR SUCCESS

1. *Ideological Diversity.* There is no monolithic "conservative" movement but rather a plethora of ideologies successfully harnessed together in a grand coalition. In the 1970s, as the New Right emerged from the discredited old right, a fragile truce was drawn among libertarians, economic conservatives, social conservatives and neoconservatives. Under the leadership of William F. Buckley Jr., editor of the influential *National Review* magazine and host of TV's *Firing Line*, tensions were negotiated and a "fusion politics" emerged that allowed for cooperation across differences. Such a truce is more easily maintained when a movement is winning, as the New Right was under President Ronald Reagan. Now, with the Bush presidency nearing its end, the fault lines are reappearing.

    The implication for progressives is that we ought to tolerate a diversity of views and think strategically about how to align them to common purpose rather than seek a homogeneity we falsely ascribe to conservatives. Conservatives also found that it's not always the most mainstream or moderate voices who win. Likewise, progressives with a more radical vision, while working collaboratively in the larger movement, must not let themselves be sidelined.

2. *Ideas, Not Messages.* To the extent that conservatives were serious about ideas—and to be sure they were and are—they started not with "messaging" or "framing,"

two strategies currently in vogue among progressives, but rather with inquiry into core beliefs about race, government, family, markets and global economic and military domination. These core beliefs were at first far outside the mainstream of accepted political discourse. But by carefully constructing an ideological blueprint for their movement (despite lack of complete buy-in from every sector), the right has been working for more than twenty-five years with a set of unifying ideological principles to which their strategists and activists return time and again. Support for "family values," limited government, a strong military, white domination and the primacy of Christianity over other religions, when combined with a will to power, have served the right well.

On the left many intellectual projects are more tactical in nature and avoid asking fundamental questions—not about how we talk but about what we actually believe. For instance, we are at our best when fighting a reactionary policy or program, such as tax cuts for the wealthy or attacks on voting rights. But progressives are not unified, or even clear, about what we affirmatively want in terms of a role for government, a just economy or rights for individuals and groups.

3. *Active Listening.* It is often noted that the structure of the conservative movement is hierarchical and that because the leadership has such a high level of control, conservative campaigns have always been well coordinated and executed with great precision. Less often noted is that their masterstroke was not that they went off in a room and decided on a few cornerstone values and then aligned their work and campaigns to speak to those values. Their genius was that they first engaged in a practice of active listening and found a core of resentment among large numbers of

Americans—about race, class, gender and sexuality—that could provide the emotional base for a new intellectual paradigm. They did this in the 1970s, at precisely the time when liberals stopped listening, presuming that the reactionary ideas of the old right were so far out of favor that only the most uninformed and backward voters supported them. Today, liberals rely heavily on polling—a shallow kind of listening—or push ideas at the country without deeply engaging with people first.

4. *The Importance of Recruitment.* Think tanks and their output of ideas, analysis and information are a necessary but not sufficient component of any effective social movement. Conservatives focused on building powerful mass-based institutions that could provide muscle for a conservative agenda, such as the National Rifle Association, the Moral Majority, the American Family Association and, later, Focus on the Family, Concerned Women for America and the Christian Coalition of America. Many of these mass-based organizations were explicitly Christian and played a vital role in recruiting evangelical and fundamentalist Christians to the New Right of the 1980s.

Further, the right's core leadership showed extraordinary creativity in exploiting new technologies. For example, Richard Viguerie pioneered the use of direct mail; Ralph Reed Jr. of the Christian Coalition developed "stealth" methods of campaigning for political office without revealing the candidates' actual right-wing agenda and used churches to mobilize voters. The right's strategists focused not only on ideas and policies but also on organizing a base and developing recruitment techniques to build the base. The contemporary right has always been clear about the importance of recruiting greater numbers to its movement. An examination of right-wing campaigns reveals that, in nearly every case, the opportunity for recruitment plays a central role in their conceptualization and execution. Progressives would make a tragic mistake by neglecting base-building in the current period.

5. *Electoral Politics as Means, Not End.* The architects of the right's rise to power did not view their project as the election of Republicans to state and federal office. They perceived the Republican Party as a tool to achieve certain ends, rather than as the end in itself; the takeover of the party was important because it would turn the country toward a reactionary agenda. That the takeover occurred is a reflection of the potency of the strategy. This is crucially important because some progressives tend to conflate the project of building a just world with the project of electing Democrats to office. Winning people over is our central task. After all, progressive advances do not always come under Democratic administrations. It was Richard Nixon, after all, who proposed a guaranteed annual income for the poor, while Bill Clinton approved time limits on welfare benefits.

It's also important to remember that the right worked at the federal, state and local levels and used both "inside" and "outside" strategies to influence the realm of political office-holding and the terrain of public opinion. No one aspect of movement-building was emphasized at the expense of others. It is that strength—approaching movement-building as a whole package—that explains much of the right's growth and effectiveness.

6. *Fearless Politics.* The right has not been afraid to propose extreme positions, knowing they will be pushed back to more moderate ones still well to the right of the status quo. We've seen this in almost every policy fight since 1980. By

boldly taking stands that are far outside the mainstream, the right has managed to pull the mainstream to the right, which is why it is now perceived as speaking for the majority. For progressives, meanwhile, timidity, ambiguity and constant compromise have not proved successful strategies; projecting a clear, principled and uncompromising voice of progressive values and policies is not only morally compelling but strategically smart.

LEARNING FROM OUR OWN HISTORY

Historically, left and liberal agendas—the New Deal, civil rights laws, the Great Society, women's advancement—have made progress when mass movements have forced change. To be sure, the ideas of John Maynard Keynes were crucial in legitimizing and pointing the way to a new form of capitalism and FDR was the right leader for the times, but the New Deal wasn't won by economic experts. It was won by ordinary people who organized to create a sense of crisis and a mandate for change.

While there is no formula for a social movement, we know that successful ones share some things in common. First, people become mobilized around issues they hold dear; at some level they share a powerful vision about what is wrong with society and how it must be improved; and they engage in lots of diverse activities not under any one leader's direct control. The resulting political motion and its effect lead to a change in attitudes, practices and public policy.

Our current infatuation with the strategies and structures of the right has led some progressives to call for a more streamlined, hierarchical movement, but this is not how we've won in the past. Progressive movements have been successful when they have not had a top-down organizational structure. Also, this analysis fails to appreciate the comprehensiveness of the right's movement-building style. And it does not reflect progressive democratic principles. Consider, for example, the civil rights movement. Despite the popular perception of the Rev. Martin Luther King Jr.'s singular importance, the movement had many sectors under many leaders, with different ideologies and different priorities—people like Septima Clark, Ella Baker and Bob Moses, all of whom believed in the centrality of developing ordinary people as agents of change rather than in charismatic leadership or coalitions of elites. The same could be said of the women's movement and the environmental movement. Progressive movements certainly need a generally agreed-upon critique of society and vision for change, as well as mechanisms for coordination. But letting a thousand flowers bloom can prove a strength, so long as power does not collect around the most "achievable" social change as opposed to the most just social change.

RACE AND SOCIAL CHANGE

A movement must have a dynamic leading edge before its positions become majority positions. Many of the progressive gains in American history were not majority agendas—ending slavery, civil rights, disability rights, AIDS advocacy and farmworker boycotts succeeded as struggles led by minorities. In some cases they were struggles led by people who weren't even enfranchised. How is that possible?

Often, deeply felt issues raised by groups whose numbers are in the minority have the power to convert, while issues that theoretically should be in everyone's interest never take hold. A necessary (though not sufficient) condition for an issue to attain broad majoritarian support is vibrant, well-organized submovements. Many of our submovements, such as the women's, environmental, LGBT and civil rights submovements, are demoralized, underfunded and increasingly influenced by their own more conservative wings. Further, the progressive movement's tendency to downplay racial issues and concerns consistently blocks our process of building from submovements' success to an effective broad progressive movement. For instance, even though African-Americans have been the core of progressive politics, it is often African-Americans who have been taken for granted and neglected by the progressive movement, which is too often white dominated and focused on issues of concern to white activists. As long as the movement fails to become more inclusive and democratic, it will continue to limp along without access to the wisdom and insight of the most vital part of its base. Race today is not simply a matter of black and white: Many other groups and movements of immigrants—Latinos, Asian/Pacific Island-Americans, Arab-Americans and Native Americans—must also have a full seat at the table. Conservatives are avidly courting these groups. When people of color look for allies to advance their issues, there is no reason to assume they will support the larger progressive movement when their issues receive only lip service and they are not widely represented in the movement's leadership and decision-making structures.

This is not only about "credibility" or "diversity." It is actually about effectiveness. The whiteness of our leadership has played out, for example, in a tendency to write off large parts of the country—including the South, the Southwest and the High Plains—which has proved politically disastrous. Further, a predominantly white leadership tends to neglect issues like immigrant rights and criminal justice because they are not pressing concerns of the "majority" of voters. The perception that an issue can't galvanize a wide majority or appeal to at least 51 percent of the electorate can sink the issue in the current climate of poll-driven strategizing. Certainly the progressive movement needs to pursue programs that knit together diverse constituencies, but even very broad issues such as healthcare or the environment will look different when they reflect the concerns of all communities.

The Role of Organizing

Some progressives consider grassroots organizing a remnant of an old style of politics no longer relevant to our media and-money-saturated times. Others think of it as an actual obstacle to the efficient, hierarchical infrastructure they idealize. But conservatives have nurtured their grassroots constituencies in civic institutions, evangelical churches and gun clubs. Organizing is central to any effective strategy for revitalizing the progressive movement.

Organizing, not to be confused with mobilizing, is ultimately what changes people's minds. Whereas mobilizing is about moving people to take certain actions (voting, lobbying policy-makers, coming out to an event or calling your Congress member on an issue pre-selected by someone else), organizing is about developing the skills, confidence and practice among ordinary people to speak out in their own voice.

What ultimately forces change is human beings seeing fellow human beings act from a place of deep conviction. That moment of recognition can occur only when people who are living with an injustice bring their experience to the public square. Of course, solidarity efforts are crucial to social change. It's hard to imagine the farmworkers, or the civil rights workers in the South, succeeding if they had failed to rouse broader sympathy throughout the country. But they were able to do this only because they spoke with an authenticity that transcended walls of race and class prejudice. No policy paper or slick message will ever replace the power of organizing.

Major changes in the social order require a leap of "nonconsent" by the governed. That might be millions of people refusing the draft, or thousands boycotting buses in Montgomery, or hundreds "dying in" to protest delays in AIDS research. While the tidal wave of conservative successes at the federal level is obvious, the less-obvious victories progressives have had in recent years are largely attributable to organizing: major new investments in affordable housing through housing trust funds, new money for transit, living-and minimum-wage laws, expansions in health coverage at the state level, more income supports for low-wage workers, education access, driver's licenses for immigrants and limits on natural resource extraction.

Organizing is, as George W. Bush might say, "hard work"— never more so than in current circumstances. Memories of successful collective struggle are fading fast among a new generation not raised with the 1960s as a backdrop. Market culture has penetrated all spheres of life, and it has reinforced deeply individualistic strains in American society. Also, pervasive economic insecurity, increasing work demands and a shredded safety net have heightened the personal costs involved.

Organizing has always had an uneasy place not only in the broader culture but also in progressive circles. It has frequently been sidelined by expert-driven advocacy or by charismatic figures who lead short-lived protest movements, and today it is at risk of being displaced by a focus on think tanks and communications strategies. Perhaps more alarming, however, is the relative decline of organizing as a strategy relative to mobilization.

For all the difficulties, progressives are engaging in some exciting experimentation with new methods of base-building appropriate to our times. Organized labor is in the throes of a debate about how to rebuild membership. There has been an explosion in community-based "worker centers" and in immigrant community organizations. And in a few states, groups are beginning to work together across issue and constituency lines to develop common long-term strategies. This success is very fragile and tentative, however, and it is still the case that organizing tends not to get the respect, attention or resources it needs from the larger progressive community.

A problem closely related to the neglect of organizing is the failure of many progressive organizations to recruit and encourage leadership from young people, especially young people of color. Young people have political, social and economic perspectives that differ from those of older (usually Baby Boomer) activists, who were shaped by the events of the 1960s and '70s. Younger activists, organizers and intellectuals will enrich the movement and take it in new directions, if given the freedom and the power to do so.

CLARIFYING BASIC PRINCIPLES

While the focus of progressive movement-building is now on creating large organizations "to scale," yet another of the movement's greatest challenges is being neglected: We are undecided on the larger principles that underlie our work for social justice. Many people don't like to do this "big picture" thinking. They prefer results-oriented activism and practical solutions. And they are correct that larger principles must be tied to people's everyday concerns and identifiable, attainable goals.

But to be successful, mass organizing must be informed by visionary principles as well as nuts-and-bolts techniques. Most bold new policy proposals grow out of the everyday work that activists in submovements do on various issues. These proposals—for example, national healthcare, full rights and services for immigrants, or replacing the racist criminal justice system—are not the polished, poll-tested, slightly left-of-center ones increasingly attractive to Democratic Party centrists. Indeed, they may seem fringe and far out of the mainstream. But they have their roots in real material conditions.

What we lack are the overarching principles to tie these proposals together. In the 1960s and '70s progressives generally agreed that government had a responsibility to defend the weak or temporarily weak, protect individual rights, provide a reasonable standard of living and regulate private enterprise to protect the public from rampant greed and criminal behavior. Battered by the right's relentless assaults on these core principles, progressive movement activists today do not have a coherent vision. Instead, we are driven by a vague sense of what a better society would look like, a recognition of how times have changed and persistent despair as we fight one defensive battle after another.

It is therefore essential that we address several fundamental questions right now: What is the role and responsibility of government? How can the racial imbalance of our movement's leadership be corrected? What role should religion play in public life? How should progressives respond to globalization? And what social issues should we identify as "bottom line"? As principles that respond to these questions emerge, we must not allow political expediency to trump creativity. The voices of people of color, and young people and women of all races must be explicitly sought out. Funding may facilitate this discussion, but it will not in itself produce a dynamic vision. Think tanks alone will not develop these principles, and framing and messaging will not substitute for them. The process of drawing out larger principles must be an organic one: a step-by-step process of slowly creating broad consensus. Here, we can learn from the right's success with active listening.

While the challenges we face are considerable, they are not insurmountable. But we must get moving so that when the tide of public opinion turns in our direction, we are not caught flatfooted, with a movement badly in need of reform and lacking the very basics needed to seize the moment and go forward. The right was ready for the backlash of the late 1970s. We must be ready for the coming backlash against the outrages of the past twenty-five years.

Thoughts on Power, Organization and Leadership

⇐

DR. MARSHALL GANZ

Dr. Martin Luther King Jr. defined power as the "ability to achieve purpose." "Whether it is good or bad," he said, "depends on the purpose." One of the key elements of power is leadership.

At least since Moses, social movement leaders—whether individuals or teams—have come from conflicted backgrounds. Moses, a Jew, the oppressed, was raised in the house of the Pharaoh, the oppressor. He struggled to link a desire for change, freeing his people, with a capacity to make change, as an Egyptian prince. Moses' reaction, killing an Egyptian taskmaster, didn't work, bringing down upon him censure from other Jews. He then fled to the desert (where you go to get your act together in the Bible) and assumed a third, quite liminal, identity as neither Jew nor Egyptian, but as the son-in-law of a Midianite priest, a shepherd.

Remaining curious, one day Moses steps off a path to attend to a strange light, a burning bush, where, it turns out, God is waiting for him. God challenges Moses to accept a call to return to Egypt, confront Pharaoh, and free his people. Moses accepts this charge only when God promises him the help of a brother, Aaron, and a sister, Miriam. He learns that he can combine his desire for change with a capacity to make change, but only by engaging with God, his family, and his people. More importantly, however, in Exodus 18, after he has brought his people out of Egypt, Moses is visited by his father-in-law, Jethro, who teaches him two things: that he has a family which requires his attention, and that he is burning himself out—and burning the people out – by trying to do all the work himself. Jethro then proposes a structure in which among every ten men, one is recruited to provide leadership, and among every then of those, one, is assigned another task, and so on. In this way, Jethro turns Moses attention to the critical role of leadership development that his movement will require if it is to grow strong.

Leading social movements requires learning to manage core tensions, tensions at the heart of what theologian Walter Brueggemann calls the "prophetic imagination": a combination of criticality (experience of the world's pain), hope (experience of the world's possibility), while avoiding being numbed by despair or deluded by optimism. The deep desire for change must be coupled with the capacity to make change. Structures must be established that create the space within which growth, creativity, and action can flourish, without slipping into the chaos of structurelessness. Leaders must also be recruited, trained, and developed on a scale required to build the relationships, sustain the motivation, do the strategizing, and carry out the actions required to achieve success.

The need for committed, hopeful leadership on a large scale is one reason that social movement leadership is often drawn from among the young (other than Moses). Dr. King was twenty-five when he was chosen to lead the bus boycott. Cesar Chavez was also twenty-five when recruited as a professional organizer and thirty-five when he initiated the farm worker movement. Some attribute the affinity of young people with social movements to "biographical availability" (having the time, but no family). Although this may hold the "costs" of activism down, it says little about the benefits. It has much more to do with Brueggemann. Young people often come of age with a critical eye, an evaluation of their parent's generation, and a hopeful heart, almost a biological necessity. As we can see from the presidential campaign of 2008, the combination can be explosive.

The Power of Story

A social movement tells a new "story." Learning how to tell that story, what I call public narrative, is an important leadership practice. Public narrative comprises three overlapping kinds of stories: a story of self, a story of us, and a story of now. A story of self communicates values that call one to action. A story of us communicates values shared by those in action. And a story of now communicates the urgent challenge to those values that requires action now.

Participating in a social movement not only often involves a re-articulation of one's story of self, us, and now, but also marks an entry into a world of uncertainty so daunting that access to sources of hope is essential. Telling one's story of self is a way to share the values that define the people we are—not as abstract principle, but as lived experience. We construct stories of self around *choice points*—moments when we faced a challenge, made a choice, experienced an outcome, and learned something. What is utterly unique about each of is not a combination of the categories (race, gender, class, profession, marital status) that include us, but rather, our journey, our way through life, our personal text from which each of us can teach.

Some of us believe our personal stories don't matter, that others won't care, or that we shouldn't talk about ourselves so much. On the contrary, if we do public work we have a responsibility to give a public account of ourselves—where we came from, why we do what we do, and where we think we're going. Stories of us express the values and the experiences shared by the "us" we are evoking at the time. They can be stories of participation in family, community, faith, organization, profession, nation, or movement. We tell these stories again and again in the form of folk sayings, songs, religious practices, and celebrations (e.g., Easter, Passover, 4th of July). And like individual stories, stories of us can inspire, teach, offer hope, advise caution, etc. We also weave new stories from old ones. The Exodus story, for example, served the Puritans when they colonized North America, but it also served Southern blacks claiming their civil rights in the freedom movement.

In a social movement, the interpretation of the movement's new experience is a critical leadership function. And, like the story of self, it is built from the choice points—the founding, the decisions made, the challenges faced, the outcomes, the lessons learned.

A story of now articulates the urgent challenge to the values that we share that demand action now. What choice must we make? What is at risk? And where's the hope? In a story of now, we are the protagonists and it is our choices that will shape the story's outcome. We must draw on our "moral sources" to respond. A most powerful articulation of a story of now was Dr. King's talk, often recalled as the "I have a dream" speech, delivered on August 23, 1963. People often forget that he preceded the dream with a challenge via white America's long overdue debt to African Americans. It was a debt that could no longer be postponed, King argued, a moment possessed of the "fierce urgency of now." If we did not act, the nightmare would grow worse, never to become the dream.

In the story of now, story and strategy overlap because a key element in hope *is a strategy*—a credible vision of *how to get from here to there*. The "choice" offered cannot be something like "we must all choose to be better people" or "we must all choose to do any one of this list of 53 things" (which makes each of them trivial). A meaningful choice is more like "do we commit to boycotting the busses until they desegregate or not?" Here, hope is specific, not abstract. When God inspired the Israelites in Exodus, he didn't offer a vague hope of "better days," but described a land "flowing with milk and honey" and what must be done to get there. A vision of hope can unfold a chapter at a time. It can begin by getting a number of people to show up at a meeting that you committed to do. You can win a "small" victory that shows change is possible. A small victory can become a source of hope if it is *interpreted* as part of a greater vision. In churches, when people have a "new story" to tell about themselves, it is often in the form of "testimony"—a person sharing an account of moving from despair to hope, the significance of the experience strengthened by the telling of it.

Through public narrative, social movement leaders—and participants—can move to action by mobilizing sources of motivation, constructing new shared individual and collective identities, and finding the courage to act.

WHO IS A LEADER?

Who is a leader? Many of us call to mind historic figures like Dr. Martin Luther King, Nelson Mandela, Jane Addams, Robert Kennedy or President Reagan. In reality, we find leaders everywhere—linking together networks through which we work to achieve common purposes. In every community, church, classroom, and organization, hundreds of people are doing the work of leadership, without which these efforts would not survive.

Although we associate leaders with certain kinds of attributes (like power), a more useful way to look at leadership is as a kind of relationship. Historian James McGregor Burns argues that leadership can be understood as a relationship that emerges from repeated "exchanges" or "transactions" between leaders and followers or constituents. Leaders can provide the resources constituents need to address their interests, while constituents can provide resources leaders need to address theirs.

What do we exchange in this kind of relationship? Constituents may get help solving a problem, a sense of empowerment, access to resources, etc. Leaders may get the same things—and something else too, something that makes us willing to accept the responsibilities that go with leadership. Dr. King described this as the "drum major instinct"—a desire to be first, to be recognized, even to be praised. As much as we may not want to admit it, this might sound familiar. Rather than condemn it—it is, after all, part of us—Dr. King argued that it could be a good thing, depending on what we do to earn the recognition we seek.

Based on this view of leadership, then, who makes leaders? Can they be self-anointed? Can I decide one day that I am a leader? Or do I earn leadership by entering into relationship with those who can make me a leader by entering into relationship with me—my constituents? There is one simple test. Do they have followers? Fine speeches, a wonderful appearance, lovely awards and excellent work aside—no constituency, no leaders. You may not agree with this, but consider it.

How Does Leadership Work?

Many of us may not want to think of ourselves as followers. While leadership is highly praised, no one says anything about being a good constituent...or citizen. I argue that voluntary associations only work when people are willing to accept roles of leadership and followership. Leading and following are not expressions of who we "are" but of what we "do" in a specific meeting, committee, project, organization, or institution. We may play a leadership role with respect to one project, and a followership role with respect to another.

Another important distinction is that between leadership and domination. Effective leaders facilitate the interdependence or collaboration that can create more "power to" based on the interests of all parties. Domination is the exercise of "power over"—a relationship that meets the interests of the "power wielder" at the expense of everyone else. Leadership can turn into domination if we fail to hold it accountable.

We are also wise to distinguish "authority" from "leadership." Authority is a "legitimacy" of command usually attached to specific social positions, offices, or roles—legitimacy supported by cultural beliefs as well as coercive resources. An organization is a way to formalize authority relations among the participants, namely people's rights and their obligations. Bureaucracies structure authority as a set of rules according to which managers direct subordinates. Markets structure authority as a set of rules according to which entrepreneurs can design incentives for persons to make enforceable choices based on their individual economic resources. Civic associations usually structure authority democratically so that leaders are accountable to the constituents whom they serve. Exercising leadership in a civic context can require more skill than in the other settings because it depends more on persuasion than on command. Most of us have been in situations in which those with authority have not earned their leadership, but try to compel cooperation based solely on their legitimacy or "power over." In these circumstances, to what extent do we think our interests are acknowledged and addressed? How does this affect our motivation and performance?

Finally, leaders should be distinguished from "activists." Hard working activists show up every day to staff the phone bank, pass out leaflets, and put up posters, making critical contribu-tions to the work of any volunteer organization. This is not the same, however, as engaging others in doing the work of the organization. Leadership is exercised through relational work.

WHAT DO LEADERS DO?

We've said a great deal about what leadership is and isn't, but what is it exactly that leaders do to earn their leadership? What is the organizational work they perform? And why is it so important?

Most of us have had lots of experience in "disorganizations." What are they like?

- They are *divided*. Factions and divisions fragment the organization and sap it of its resources.

- They are *confused*. Each person has a different story about what's going on. There is a lot of gossip, but not very much good information.

- They are *passive*. Most "members" do very little, so one or two people do most of the work.

- They are *reactive*. They are always trying to respond to some unanticipated new development.

- They are *inactive*. No one comes to meetings. No one shows up for activities.

- They *drift*. Since there is little purposefulness to meetings, actions, or decisions, things "drift" from one meeting to the next.

Being part of a disorganization can be discouraging and demotivating, making us ask ourselves why we're involved at all.

On the other hand, some of us may have had experience with organizations that really work.

- They are *united*. They have learned to manage their differences well enough that they can unite to accomplish the purposes for which they were formed. Differences are openly debated, discussed, and resolved.

- They share *understanding*. There is a widely shared understanding of what's going on, what the challenges are, what the program is and why what is being done had to be done.

- People *participate*. Lots of people in the organization are active—not just going to meetings, but getting the work of the organization done.

- They take *initiative*. Rather than reacting to whatever happens in their environment, individuals are proactive, and act upon their environment.

- They *act*. People do the work they must to make things happen.

- They share a sense of *purpose*. There is purposefulness about meetings, actions, and decisions, and a sense of forward momentum as work gets done.

So what makes the difference? Why are some groups disorganizations and other groups organizations? It is the quality of the work leaders do within them that makes groups work.

- Leaders turn division into solidarity by building, maintaining, and developing *relationships* among those who form the organization.

- Leaders turn confusion into understanding by facilitating *interpretation* of what is going on with the work of the organization.

- Leaders turn passivity into participation by *motivation* by inspiring people to commit to the action required if the group's goals are to be accomplished.

- Leaders turn reaction into initiative by *strategizing*—thinking through how the organization can use its resources to achieve its goals.

- Leaders turns inaction into action by *mobilizing* people

to turn their resources into specific actions by means which they can achieve their goals.

- Leaders transforms drift into purpose by accepting *responsibility* for doing the leadership work which must be done if the group is to succeed, and challenging others to accept their responsibilities as well.

LEADERSHIP DEVELOPMENT

Developing a leadership rich organization not only requires learning to delegate. It also requires a conscious strategy for identifying leaders (opportunities for leaders to emerge), recruiting leaders (opportunities for leadership to be earned), and developing leaders (opportunities for leaders to grow).

Identifying leaders requires looking for them. Who are people with followers? Who brings others to the meetings? Who encourages others to participate? Who attracts others to working with them? Who do other people tell you to "look for?" Saul Alinsky writes about community networks knit together by "native" leaders—people who take the responsibility for helping a community do its work out of their homes, small businesses, neighborhood hangouts, etc. These people can be found coaching athletic teams, organizing little leagues, serving in their churches, and surfacing in other informal "schools" of leadership.

Although leading is a matter of "doing" and not "being," there are some ways of being that can help you lead. It is hard for a person who has not learned to be a *good listener* to become an effective leader—you have to understand the interests of your constituency if you are to help them act on their interests. Listening means learning to attend to feelings—*empathy*—as well as to ideas, because the way we feel about things affects our actions more than what we think about them.

Curiosity helps us see the novel as interesting rather than threatening, enabling us to learn how to face the new challenges that are always a part of organizational life. A good *imagination* helps because strategizing is a matter of imagining different futures and possible ways to get to them. A sense of *humor* helps you from taking yourself and your troubles too seriously, and helps keep things in perspective. A *healthy ego* is very important—arrogance and a wish to dominate others are usually the sign of a weak ego constantly in need of reassurance. Leadership also requires courage—the willingness to take risks, make choices, and accept the consequences.

Recruiting leaders requires giving people an opportunity to earn leadership. Since followers create leaders, they can't appoint themselves and you can't appoint them. What you can do is create opportunities for people to accept the responsibilities of leadership and support them in learning how to fulfill these responsibilities. If you have to get the word out for a meeting, you can get three of your friends to help you pass out leaflets in the one day, or you can find one or two people who will take responsibility for recruiting five other people to attend. They earn their leadership by bringing the people to the meeting.

Developing leaders requires structuring the work of the organization so it affords as many people as possible the opportunity to learn to lead—delegation. Distributing the leaflets through committees, for example, shares the responsibility for engaging others with many people. It is true that organizing the work in this way can be risky. You may delegate to the wrong people; they may let you down, etc. But as Moses learned from Jethro, if you fear delegating, the strength of the community is stifled and can never grow. But you can do things to increase the chances of success. Leadership training sessions help clarify what is expected of leaders in your organization, gives people the confidence to accept leadership responsibilities, and expresses the value your organization places on leadership development.

LEADERSHIP TEAM OR "LONE RANGER"

The most successful organizers are those who form a leadership team with whom to work early on in their campaign. It can be a mistake, however, to recruit people to act as an "organizing committee" too early, especially if you are not careful to recruit people drawn from the constituency whom that community views as leaders or, at least, potential leaders. Nevertheless, the sooner you have a team of people with whom to work, however, the sooner the "I" of the organizer becomes the "we" of the new organization. One you have formed a leadership team you can more easily establish a rhythm of regular meetings, clear decisions, and visible accountability that will help make things actually happen. You don't build an organization of 500 people by recruiting them all yourself. You build it by finding people willing and able to commit to help building it with you.

CONCLUSION

Although identifying, recruiting and developing leaders is critical to the capacity—or power—of most organizations, it is the particular focus of organizers whose work is to be leaders of leaders. The primary responsibility of an organizer is to develop the leadership capacities of others and, in this way, of the organizations through which their constituents act on their common interests.

MARRIAGE EQUALITY IN MASSACHUSETTS: A PROGRESSIVE VICTORY

⇐

LEO MALEY

On November 18, 2003, by a vote of 4 to 3, the Massachusetts Supreme Judicial Court ruled in *Goodridge v. Department of Public Health* that the state constitution did not permit "the creation of second-class citizens," and that therefore, Massachusetts could no longer ban same-sex civil marriages. The first same-sex marriage licenses were issued 180 days after the ruling, on the fiftieth anniversary of the *Brown v. Board of Education* decision ending legal segregation of the public schools. Celebratory crowds gathered at city and town halls across the state as over 1,000 same-sex couples wed for the occasion. Over 10,000 gay and lesbian couples have been married to date—and marriage equality is now an established fact of life in Massachusetts.

The back-story of this historic civil and human rights victory is the role of over 1,000 clergy—and numerous laypersons—who, in publicly supporting marriage equality, powerfully reframed the same-sex marriage debate in a way that helped lead to this major progressive achievement. However, the historic *Goodridge* decision is not the achievement I am talking about. Instead, the victory to which religious progressives contributed so significantly was the dramatic showdown vote in the state legislature in 2006 that headed off a state-wide ballot question designed to undo *Goodridge* and thus write discrimination into the Massachusetts constitution. *This* success story should embolden and inspire progressive religious activists as a model for organizing on this issue over the long haul, as well as informing our thinking about a broader and more politically dynamic Religious Left.

CHANGING THE CONSTITUTION

Even as progressives celebrated the first same-sex marriages in 2004, the opposition was already mobilizing to amend the state constitution to forbid future marriages. Fortunately, it is not easy to change the Massachusetts constitution. There are two ways to do it. One, a majority of legislators can vote (during two successive two-year legislative sessions) to put an amendment question on the ballot, whereupon it must be approved by the voters. Two, an amendment can be initiated by petition of the voters. If an amendment originates by petition, a mere one-forth of the state legislature must vote in favor of the amendment (also during two legislative sessions) for the question to move to the ballot.

In the spring of 2004, some legislators proposed a constitutional amendment that would have outlawed same-sex marriages, but sanctioned civil unions. This would have been a major step backward for the marriage equality movement. The proposal passed the first of its two required constitutional conventions by a vote of 105 to 92, but lost by a vote of 157 to 39 when it came up a second time in the fall of 2005. However, the real test for proponents of marriage equality was yet to come.

That fall, a coalition supported by the Catholic Church, Focus on the Family, and its state political affiliate the Massachusetts Family Institute gathered 170,000 signatures (almost three times the number needed) to restrict marriage to opposite-sex couples. On January 2, 2007, days before the 2005-06 legislative was to end, 62 out of 200 legislators—twelve more than the 25 percent needed—voted in favor of the amendment. But, just five months later, on June 14, 2007, by a vote of 151 to 45, legislators voted against sending the question to the ballot in 2008. The ballot initiative was dead, and marriage equality in Massachusetts was assured for the foreseeable future. Needless to say, this win did not come easily.

MassEquality, a coalition of state and national organizations that formed in the late 1990s to oppose conservative efforts to pass discriminatory "defense of marriage" legislation, took the lead in the wake of the opposition to *Goodridge*. The group developed an impressive statehouse lobbying effort, as well as a first-rate field organization. This dual approach was important, because the anti-marriage-equality forces mounted vigorous efforts to increase their numbers in the legislature (the votes of only one-quarter of the legislature was needed to go the ballot initiative route).

In addition, the Republican Party actively recruited conservative candidates to run against pro-equality legislators. However, in the legislative elections of 2004 and 2006, something remarkable happened: Every pro-equality legislator was reelected, several anti-equality incumbents were defeated, and a number of pro-equality candidates were elected for the first time. All this was thanks in large part to MassEquality and the Mass Alliance (a broad-based multi-issue progressive electoral coalition). To top it all off, Deval Patrick, an articulate pro-equality candidate was elected governor in 2006 in place of the retiring Mitt Romney, a vocal opponent of marriage equality. In just two years, marriage equality had gone from a potential liability to being a clear political plus for anyone running for a legislative seat or for state-wide office.

Progressives—both inside and outside of Massachusetts—have yet to come to terms with the enormity of this political shift, the possibility that it might be replicated in other states, and particularly, the critical role progressive clergy and laity played in this landmark civil rights victory, which has served as a catalyst for wider progressive electoral victories.

ENTER THE RCFM

Not to be overlooked in this story was the role of the Religious Coalition for the Freedom to Marry (RCFM), which began in 1998 as an annual interfaith gathering of clergy committed to the idea that gay and lesbian couples should have the same right to marry as heterosexual couples. RCFM considered marriage equality to be "one of the most pressing civil rights issues in America today" as well as a matter of religious liberty.

With the decision in the landmark *Goodridge* case looming, in 2003 activists involved in the litigation asked if RCFM could increase its organizing efforts and play a more public role once the legal decision had been rendered. After the court decision, RCFM held a public worship service and, most importantly, intensified efforts to increase the number of clergy who signed the group's "Declaration of Religious Support for the Freedom of Same-Gendered Couples to Marry." The Declaration stated that "a denial of civil recognition dishonors the religious convictions of those communities and clergy who do officiate at, and bless, same-gender marriages," and that "the state may not favor the convictions of one religious group over another to deny individuals their fundamental right to marry and have those marriages recognized by civil law." Signers of the Declaration committed "to public action, visibility, education, and mutual support in the service of the right and freedom to marry." Newspaper advertisements containing the names of clergy signers of the Declaration ran in several Massachusetts newspapers.

RCFM also encouraged clergy and laity to tell personal stories that emphasized the themes of civil rights (equality before the law) and religious freedom (the state not establishing one religious perspective over another). Many of these stories—several quite moving—were collected in *People of Faith Testimony: Rejoicing in Marriage Equality*, a book that was delivered to all 200 state legislators in 2006. In addition, a pamphlet titled, "Neither Fair Nor Just: Why We Don't Vote on Civil Rights," was distributed in synagogues and churches.

In June 2006, RCFM publicly confronted what it called the "bigotry espoused in the name of faith," by releasing an open letter that charged the Catholic Church with "religious discrimination" for trying to deny legal recognition to marriages conducted by clergy of other faiths. (Keep in mind that Catholics comprise fully half of the population in Massachusetts, and over two-thirds of state legislature.) The letter declared that "By proclaiming homosexuality and same-sex unions to be universally immoral and worthy of second-class status under state law, you are sending a message that our faith communities are immoral. You are harming us and our families and your own faithful as well."

RCFM also gathered thousands of signatures from pro-equality Catholics on a "Roman Catholic Statement Supporting Marriage Equality for Same-Sex Couples in Massachusetts" which emphasized the "danger of one religious tradition or doctrine dominating another," and affirmed the constitutional principle of the separation of church and state. The Statement recalled that Roman Catholics were once denied civil rights, argued that Catholic social justice teachings called for respect, "not merely tolerance," and reminded the public that "same-sex civil marriage does not in any way coerce any religious faith or tradition to change its beliefs or doctrine."

RCFM's challenge to the Catholic Church's anti-equality stance was critical. And the courage and integrity of the religious leaders who stood up for what they believed, and effectively organized on behalf of their convictions, made a crucial difference in preserving marriage equality in Massachusetts.

In 2006, Arline Isaacson, lobbyist for the Massachusetts Gay and Lesbian Political Caucus and one of the state's key strategists for the marriage equality struggle, summarized the important role RCFM had played, telling a newspaper that the organization "produced critically important support to legislators struggling with theological and cultural questions about marriage by providing two things for lawmakers—a comfort zone based on traditional theology and a political cultural framework to consider the issue that never existed before." Isaacson continued by saying that RCFM had "changed the nature of the debate from religion versus gays to religion versus religion. So we can now forcefully assert that denying us marriage rights is the equivalent of choosing one set of religious views over another. And no legislator ever wants to be caught favoring one religious tradition over another, debating over whose interpretation of God is the right one."

LESSONS

The main lesson that can be ascertained from the marriage equality fight in Massachusetts is that if progressives leave the playing field to the Religious Right and its allies, they are in essence forfeiting the game. However, when progressives play—and play to win—they can accomplish much.

A winning strategy for the Religious Left on the issue of marriage equality—which can be extended to other progressive issues as well—can be distilled into three main points:

1. Clergy and laity should not avoid taking a public stand in favor of marriage equality because it is "controversial" or because it might upset a few members of one's congregation. It is not only the right thing to do and politically important, but interviews with pro-equality clergy suggest that personal—and congregational—affirmations of marriage equality contribute to a deeper personal religious understanding, and also to congregational growth and renewal.

2. Winning requires hard work. In the case of marriage

equality, public opinion had to be changed, and legislators had to be persuaded or replaced. In addition, there were the usual ideological, tactical, and personality issues with which to contend. But, in the end, people worked hard, played smart, and kept the faith.

3. Start small; start now. The handful of Jewish, Protestant, and Unitarian Universalist clergy who started RCFM in the 1990s had no idea that marriage equality would so quickly become a defining issue in state politics. However, when the *Goodridge* decision came, they were ready to play a critical role. Religious progressives should take heart from their victory, and learn from their example.

THE ORGANIZING MODEL OF WE BELIEVE OHIO

⇐

ANASTASIA PANTSIOS

The Reverend Rod Parsley, pastor of the World Harvest mega-church in suburban Columbus, Ohio, was feeling his oats after the 2004 election. He had stumped the state with Ohio Secretary of State Ken Blackwell on behalf of an amendment to the state's constitution banning gay marriage, and the issue had carried with more than 60 percent of the vote. The latest item on Parsley's agenda was getting Blackwell elected as Ohio's governor in 2006. Parsley and fellow suburban Columbus megachurch pastor Russell Johnson of Fairfield Christian Church, geared up, with Johnson spearheaded the Ohio Restoration Project, a group that aimed to enlist thousands of "Patriot Pastors" to register half a million new conservative Christian voters. Parsley's Reformation Ohio was doing similar work through its Center for Moral Clarity.

However, Parsley's bluster and overt partisanship had an unintended effect: it aroused people in Ohio who did not share his view of what it meant to be a person of faith. This led to the formation of We Believe Ohio, a loose network of pastors, rabbis, imams and other religious and lay leaders of various faiths which was founded to provide a counterbalance to the very vocal pastors on the religious right.

Tim Ahrens of Columbus's First Congregational Church, who was the driving force behind the formation of We Believe Ohio, recalled a pivotal moment that took place in mid-October, 2005:

"I sat down over a nice cup of coffee on a Saturday morning and opened the paper and read that Rod Parsley and his group were on the Statehouse steps saying, and I quote, 'We are locked, loaded and firing on Ohio.' My next question was 'What does that have to do with Jesus?' [Parsley's] on our Statehouse steps and a lot of us took the ostrich approach: 'If we keep doing our good works and organizing for justice in Columbus, this guy will just go away.' But it dawned on me that we needed a different response. We wanted to have another voice in the public square, and to end the monologue and have a dialogue."

Ahrens called up all the Christian pastors he knew, rounding up about fifty for a mid-November meeting. At that gathering, the group decided it needed to reach outside the Christian community and bring other religious leaders into the discussion.

An article written about the meeting by First Congregational Church's Denny Mahoney appeared in the *Columbus Dispatch* on November 18, 2005 and attracted the attention of the Washington, DC-based 501(c)(3) group Faith in Public Life, which was forming at the same time with the intention of being a communications and networking resource for faith groups that "share a call to pursue justice and the common good." Reverend Jennifer Butler, the executive director of Faith in Public Life, and director of communications strategy Katie Barge made contact with the fledgling Ohio group in order to figure out how the two organizations could work together.

"We were founded to be a resource center for faith groups working for compassion, justice and the common good," said Barge.

"We were looking to get involved in Ohio even before Faith in Public Life actually launched, before We Believe Ohio launched, when we were a nascent organization. [Butler] was interviewing people to get a sense of the religious landscape. She heard about the Rev. Tim Ahrens in Columbus and ended up speaking with him. It seemed like something good was happening there so she ended up sending me down to Ohio, to meet with the folks there. And we ended up working together because there was so much energy around what was going to be an official media launch."

With Faith in Public Life offering input on honing its message and organizing its debut, We Believe Columbus launched in March, 2006 with more than 100 people in attendance at the launch event.

We Believe Ohio is designed as a peer-to-peer (mainly) clergy network to bring leaders of various faiths together to work on peace and social justice initiatives and to provide a media voice to counterbalance that of the religious right. In 2007, the group publicly called for civility in the budget-making process between the new Democratic governor and the Republican-majority legislature. In May 2007, it sponsored a lobby day in Columbus on issues related to housing, education and health care. In the fall of 2007, with a vitriolic Republican primary in Ohio's 5th district to replace Congressman Paul Gillmor, who had died suddenly, We Believe Ohio announced a "Sleazefree Ohio" campaign, which urged candidates of all parties to sign a pledge promising to stick to issues and eschew name-calling.

The group's next priority was working on a response to initiatives for equal opportunity for all people, acknowledging that, although group members have different beliefs on homosexuality, all agree that equal treatment under the law is a civil rights and justice issue. (In fact, individual members of We Believe Ohio may be politically or theologically conservative; their agreement stems from their belief that issues like gay marriage and abortion have crowded out important faith-based discussions of issues like poverty and social and economic justice.)

We Believe Ohio's greatest success to date has been to start conversations among in-state progressive faith groups about building coalitions behind social-justice legislation. In Columbus, it has worked with the voter-mobilization group Faith Vote Columbus, an affiliate of the Industrial Areas Foundation, and B.R.E.A.D., an association of congregations which describes itself as "a vehicle for congregations to practice justice by joining together large numbers of people that can hold public officials accountable."

To date, We Believe's greatest liability is its limited funding, which is far overshadowed by the congregations and organizations on the right. Faith in Public Life has provided some resources in the areas of communications and web-site building, and Reverend Butler facilitated a September, 2006 retreat for forty of We Believe's clergy and lay leaders. But since the group doesn't accept money from corporate sponsors, can't raise the millions of dollars that megachurch collection plates generate, hasn't hired professional fundraisers to solicit donations or go after grants, and doesn't have staff or field organizers, its ability to do community organizing or to mobilize the numbers that someone like Parsley can bring to the Statehouse steps is still lacking.

In 2007, Faith in Public Life and We Believe Ohio joined with Susan Thistlethwaite of the Chicago Theological Seminary to start the process of exporting the We Believe model to other states. In May, a meeting was held at CTS with representatives from groups in Michigan, Pennsylvania, Arkansas Colorado and South Carolina to share what We Believe Ohio had done and to do media and community organization training.

The follow-up to that gathering was handled by Ron Stief, who was involved in Faith in Public Life's founding and came on board in September, 2007 as director of organizing. By mid-2008, the Chicago training had led to the launch of We Believe Colorado in June, with Pennsylvania and Arkansas still in discussions about the format such a group might take in those states. Colorado provided fertile territory, Stief said, because it had long been home to extremist right-wing religious groups such as James Dobson's Colorado Springs-based Focus on the Family, and was also ground zero for such right-wing initiatives as TABOR (a tax-and-spending cap) which has stifled the state's economy. As with We Believe Ohio, the Colorado group includes a range of faith groups, including Jewish and Islamic groups.

Although Faith in Public Life offers hands-on organizing assistance, each group it supports is independent and develops its own priorities based on local realities. "It's a network, not an organization," Stief said of FiPL. "We use open-source organizing. We want it to be replicated. FiPL isn't trying to build chapters. What we're trying to do is strengthen local leadership from where they are and the organizations they already sit in, to get solutions to some of the issues we care about. The local groups can call themselves whatever they want. Colorado just happened to call themselves we Believe Colorado. Another group in Pennsylvania is looking at the model. We don't want FiPL to be name of any of the group."

Given its lack of resources to organize on a full-time basis (the group is directed informally by a steering committee of clergy), the main impact of We Believe Ohio has been to contribute to a growing awareness that not all faith-based groups or people of faith are focused on the narrow set of issues (abortion, gays) that have commonly been described in the media as animating "values" voters. Faith in Public Life has helped to amplify that voice—and hopes to amplify the voice of other such groups—with resources such as its *Faith in Politics Daily,* a free-source round-up of several breaking faith-related stories, and its online map of over 3,000 progressive faith organizations, a resource Stief describes as "an online sourcebook for reporters and organizers. Reporters, if there's a story and they want to get a perspective in South Dakota, they can go to that map, and see who can comment. We give visibility to things that are already going on."

"In 2006, there was one religious voice being heard in the public square," says Tim Ahrens. "That voice was coming from Rod Parsley and Russell Johnson and the Patriot Pastors. We said, there are others of us here. That is not a small step. Sometimes I look back and think we haven't done enough. But that is not a small thing when the momentum and the money were swinging to the religious right."

THREE WHEELS THAT NEED NOT BE
REINVENTED

⇦

FREDERICK CLARKSON

The main reason why the Religious Right became powerful is not what most people may think. Some would undoubtedly point to the powerful communications media. Others might identify charismatic leaders, the development of "wedge issues," or even changes in evangelical theology in the latter part of the twentieth century that supported, and even demanded political action. All of these and more, especially taken together, were important factors. But the main reason for the Religious Right's rise to power has been its capacity for political action, particularly electoral politics.

On the Religious Left, many of the ingredients are present for a more dynamic movement. But the ingredient that is most remarkably lacking is the one that made the Religious Right powerful: a capacity for electoral politics. Indeed, there has never been anything on the Religious Left on the scale of Jerry Falwell's Moral Majority, Pat Robertson's Christian Coalition, or any of the dozens of significant Religious Right groups (such as the state political affiliates of Focus on the Family) that have had any significant national or regional electoral muscle. Electoral politics is, of course, not a panacea. But no one who is serious about the distribution of power in this constitutional democracy can expect to accomplish very much without a broad electoral strategy and the capacity to carry it out. That is why I think that the Religious Left, in order to create a more just society, is going to need to take electoral politics more seriously—and not just as a religious auxiliary of the Democratic Party.

Electoral politics is not only a defining activity of constitutional democracy in America—it is the principal avenue for gaining sufficient popular power to improve the lives of the poor and the marginalized via government and public policy, as well as to address the entire constellation of progressive concerns. And by electoral politics, I do not mean merely voting; I mean actually mastering the mechanics of electoral politics and sustaining a permanent activist presence in our communities, and building organizations to sustain it. Such organizations—like those of the Religious Right—must be unconnected to the fortunes of one or another candidate and be much more than a shell group (or group of shells) to be revved-up only in the run up to an election.

Part of the genius of the Religious Right, particularly the once-formidable Christian Coalition, is the way they work across election cycles to build their capacity to affect electoral outcomes; recruiting, training and organizing support for candidates, particularly in party primaries for offices at all levels. They also systematically register like minded-voters and have developed the capacity to turn them out on Election Day. And they keep good data bases. In other words, they have mastered the contemporary tools and mechanics of electoral democracy.

Again, there is nothing remotely like this on the Religious Left—which frankly just does not do democracy as well as the Religious Right. I think that acknowledging this simple fact of American political life is a necessarily prerequisite to opening-up the necessary conversation about what it will take for the Religious Left to be better able to live up to the promise of its most prophetic and pragmatic leaders.

People can write letters, organize phone banks, lobby, protest, and conduct prayer vigils—but what if those who hold elected office are not interested in listening? That is perhaps the central question of constitutional democracy. And to ask the question is to suggest the answer. Obviously, it is far better to have people in office with whom we agree (or mostly agree) than people who don't. So the answer is to elect better public officials.

But how do we do this? Fortunately, it is not necessary to completely reinvent the wheel. What follows are brief descriptions of three kinds of "wheels" that I think are adaptable to different sectors of the progressive religious community around the country.

First, a little background. I live in Massachusetts, arguably the most Democratic state in the country. Currently, the entire Congressional delegation is Democratic, as are 175 out of the 200 state legislators. But the overwhelming numbers of Democrats in the legislature has not translated into progressive public policy as much as one might think, as conservative Democrats largely held sway in the legislature for decades and enacted few of the progressive planks in the party platform.

But that is changing. Progressives have significantly increased their numbers in the legislature and in statewide office over the course of several election cycles, thanks in considerable part to three innovative organizations that each feature distinctly successful models of organizing: Neighbor-to-Neighbor, Boston Vote, and Progressive Democrats of Massachusetts.

NEIGHBOR-TO-NEIGHBOR

The Boston-based Neighbor-to-Neighbor (N2N) organization began in 1996 after an analysis showed that forty-seven House districts should have had more progressive representatives than they did. Using grassroots organizing, leadership development, electoral

campaigns, legislative lobbying and voter registration and education, the group "built power" in low-income and working-class
communities. As a result, Neighbor-to-Neighbor has a remarkable record of turning around the problem of low levels of voter
participation in lower-income urban communities. For example,
in 2002 the group dramatically increased voter turnout in low-income precincts of several cities, including increases of 185 percent
in Salem; 900 percent in Lynn; 210 percent in Leominster; 589
percent in Fitchburg; and 131 percent in Worcester. This contributed to the election of progressive candidates as well as two progressive Democratic members of Congress, Rep. James McGovern
of Worcester and Rep. John Tierney of Gloucester. Sustained
organizing in Worcester, Salem and Holyoke was a deciding factor in the 2003 election of progressive, Latino city councilors in
those cities. "Since 1997 we have unelected or swung a large bloc
of the target legislators," former Executive Director Harris Gruman told me in 2003. He said another twenty-five were needed to
make the House a reasonably progressive place, but that that goal
was in sight. "There is nothing quite like the persuasive impact of
seeing your colleagues go down." Since then, about a dozen more
progressives have been elected to the legislature, and the tone has
dramatically changed.

N2N's success is based on "targeted organizing" around what
it calls "The Working Family Agenda." This agenda comprises
"good jobs, education and training, affordable child care, health
care and housing, and a welfare safety net." Their methods include
year-round intensive voter contact and issue mobilization across
the election cycle, followed by personal, telephone and mail contact
during electoral campaigns. "With year-round voter engagement,"
Gruman said, "you change the equation dramatically. Most people
don't pay much attention to politics until the presidential campaign
comes around."

PROGRESSIVE DEMOCRATS OF MASSACHUSETTS

Progressive Democrats of Massachusetts (PDM) grew out of the 2002 gubernatorial campaign of former U.S. Secretary of Labor Robert Reich, whose spirited but unsuccessful bid for the Democratic nomination attracted thousands of previously alienated and uninvolved progressives. After Republican Mitt Romney defeated Democratic regular Shannon O'Brien in the general election, some Reich supporters decided to create a permanent electoral organization to continue to invite progressives into the party, and train leaders and activists with the goal of making the Democratic Party a far more progressive place.

Organizing committees were soon formed in a dozen towns and cities. Since then, some groups have come and gone and new ones have formed, as is the nature of politics and organizing. As of this writing, there are active groups centered in Gloucester, Lexington, Arlington, Amherst/Northampton, Brookline, the Berkshires, South Hadley/Holyoke and Chelmsford. PDM is continuously sustaining and growing a statewide network of experienced and accomplished electoral activists with a history of working effectively together. PDM has also played a decisive role in key state legislative campaigns, and its activists were an early and integral part of the field organization for a long-shot reform candidate for governor—Deval Patrick—who was elected in 2006.

The secret of the group's success to date is the organizing method of founding board member Marshall Ganz, a former top organizer for the United Farm Workers who teaches organizing at Harvard's Kennedy School of Government. Ganz's method focuses on one-on-one recruiting, the development of personal political relationships and leadership training—all aimed at expanding the pool of progressive voters and activists. His method builds on the cumulative experiences and best practices of social justice organizing from the labor, women's and civil rights movement, among many others.

PDM says of itself that by organizing "as a progressive voice in the party, we believe that we can make a far greater difference than by merely becoming party activists. PDM also believes that third parties and third party candidates unnecessarily divide progressives against themselves and thereby lend support to the Republican Party rather than bringing about needed political change. We hope that one result of our activism will be that more people will become inspired to become deeply involved in the life of the Democratic Party." Or as N2N's Harris Gruman put it, "If we are going to have a political party, it needs to mean something."

PDM and N2N do differ in several important respects. N2N has paid staff and organizes primarily in urban, low-income communities of color. PDM is based primarily (but not exclusively) in white middle class and college communities, and operates on an almost all volunteer basis. Many of PDM's volunteers are able to travel and assist in targeted races outside of their own districts. While these organizations developed separately, they are close allies. They recognize that building for power takes time, patience and hard work regardless of town or constituency. As a general rule, people's personal and group political behavior changes slowly – therefore a certain kind of patience is a necessary element of political maturity, even amidst the urgency of the issues of the day and the tumult of electoral politics and the necessary impatience in the face of indifference and inaction.

The progressive advances of recent years did not occur out the blue. The progressive resurgence in the state showed itself long before the catalytic candidacies of Robert Reich, Howard Dean, Deval Patrick, and Barack Obama. PDM and N2N are also members of the Mass Alliance and its predecessor, the statewide Commonwealth Coalition, comprising progressive unions, women and environmental groups that engaged in more traditional electoral campaigns; trained thousands of activists; and helped forge a progressive caucus of state legislators. PDM and N2N capitalized on these trends—and encouraged, expanded, and organized them.

BOSTON VOTE

A different kind of model with electoral implications was pioneered by Boston Vote, a 501(c)(3) nonprofit, tax-exempt organization founded in 1999 to encourage social service and other nonprofit agencies in low-income urban areas to register their clients to vote and help to turn them out on Election Day. By definition, Boston Vote is non-partisan, but it offers a kind of model that allows progressive social service agencies and religious organizations to integrate voter registration and mobilization into their existing programs. Boston Vote and several participating agencies received major foundation funding to develop a civic education program to increase voter participation among low-income communities of color. Of the 140 groups in the program, George Pillsbury of Boston Vote told me in 2003, about fifty were very active. The organization has since developed basic materials and low-to-no-cost training to help nonprofits register people to vote, and to mobilize others, as well as to eliminate barriers to participation to a variety of disadvantaged groups.

"We've gotten out the message that these non-profits really depend on voter turnout in order to get their voices heard, to fulfill their missions and to receive continued funding," Pillsbury said. "What progressives have done over 30 years is set up good non-profit organizations that have grown out of various pieces of liberal legislation—organizations that the communities fundamentally trust."

Their efforts to ratchet-up voter participation in the communities they serve, according to Pillsbury, were responsible for the reelection of Felix Arroyo, a Latino Boston councilor. "Voter turnout in the black, Asian and Latino communities went up 80 percent, while [turnout in] the white communities went down 12 percent," Pillsbury said. "Felix Arroyo came in second in a field of 5 [for four seats in 2003], because our precincts turned out." Since then, the group has gone statewide and is now called Mass Vote.

NAVIGATING THE NON-PROFIT TAX CODE

Finally, it is important to underscore that churches and service agencies know that the IRS proscribes electioneering as a condition of federal tax-exemption, and they quite properly do not want to undermine their mission by getting in trouble. Fortunately, the rules governing what is and is not permissible are not only fair and reasonable, but are surprisingly comprehensible, and the kinds of activities encouraged by Mass Vote are well-within the IRS rules. This is the stuff of basic empowerment in electoral democracy, as the much-honored but too often forgotten African-American Civil Rights movement taught us.

What Mass Vote teaches tax-exempt groups to do within the law, is different than becoming a lobbying group or an electoral organization. That said, lobbying and electoral organizations are necessary too—but are necessarily separate. Thus, leaders of a more politically dynamic Religious Left will need to not only master the mechanics of electoral politics, but the non-profit tax code as well. And they will have to create new organizations to carry out different tasks. I know that this may seem daunting. But the good news is that these wheels need not be reinvented, as there are lots of people and organizations with the relevant knowledge and experience to draw upon. We can learn and master the tools handed to us by the generations that have brought our constitutional democracy this far. If we do, a vibrant and politically dynamic Religious Left can be a powerful part of the coalition necessary to bend the arc of history towards what Martin Luther King Jr. called justice.

This essay was adapted from the article, "Putting the Mass in Massachusetts," which was published in the December 15, 2003 issue of In These Times magazine.

Using New Media to Strengthen the Religious Left

⇐

SHELBY MEYERHOFF AND SHAI SACHS

The Religious Left is a diverse movement that includes individuals, entrepreneurs, 501(c)(3) nonprofits, social justice groups within congregations, and advocacy organizations. While each of these groups may have different resources, missions, and target audiences, they all can benefit from a greater awareness—and more effective use—of new media. By "new media," we mean everything from blogs and text-messaging to social networking tools and media sharing sites. Much of what is now available is not only user friendly, but also comes with low or no cost attached, thus opening up unprecedented possibilities for the Religious Left.

We must seize this opportunity to shape public perceptions of religious and political issues, build a larger network of supporters, and mobilize for more powerful social change. New media tools are perfectly suited to the task of networking and mobilizing diverse communities and individuals into a larger movement. Anyone with an Internet connection and sufficient know-how can participate, and new media can quickly turn a casual reader into an activist. This allows us to take a, powerful, bottom-up approach to movement building.

In the examples below, we take the perspective of an organization or an individual wishing to communicate with an audience. From this starting point, activists can create an effective online strategy to promote the larger vision of a diverse and engaged Religious Left.

One of the advantages of new media is that it allows the Religious Left to counter the influence of the conservative media. We already have examples to prove it. Blogs like *Daily Kos* and *The Huffington Post* have audiences that rival that of *Fox News*. Exciting new technologies will soon make it possible for anyone to watch Internet video on a normal television set. Many social networking sites (as we'll see below) are extending their reach onto cell phones and other mobile devices. Another advantage is that new media provides opportunities for users of different ages, faiths, and backgrounds to share ideas and build relationships.

In this essay, we provide a brief introduction to the exciting range of new media tools available to the Religious Left, with examples of specific services which organizations can use to get started, as well as describing some of the most important characteristics of each service. We've also divided new media into two categories—content-creation tools and content-promotion tools. To some extent this is an arbitrary distinction. You could argue that all of these tools can be used for both content creation and promotion; but each has, particular strengths in our experience, and that is why we organize them as we do, as a guide for people thinking about crafting a balanced communications strategy.

CONTENT-CREATION

- *Blogs. (Tools: Blogger and Wordpress)*

Blogs are popular because they are easy to set up and administer (although a successful blog requires a significant investment of time spent updating content and networking with other bloggers). They are also easy for readers to access (all that's required is Internet access and a computer), and allow readers to communicate with one another and with the author through comments. Group blogs are websites that allow multiple users to create blogs, as well as comment on and rate one another's blogs. Usually a group blog focuses on a specific topic, providing a gathering place for participants with shared interests. A great example of this is *Street Prophets* where writers from many different faith traditions discuss progressive politics.

* *Podcasts and vlogs. (Tools: iTunes, Miro)*
Podcasts and vlogs are similar to blogs, in that they are chronologically-organized, regularly-updated displays of content, with a space for comments. In the case of podcasts, the content is an audio file; in the case of vlogs, the content is a video. With software like iTunes or Miro, the audience can easily subscribe to such lists. When listeners subscribe to podcasts, they can download the latest video or audio file onto an iPod, and play it at any time, such as during their morning and evening commute.

* *Content management systems. (Tools: Drupal, Joomla, and Plone)*
A content management system is a software product which allows you to easily edit the content on your website. Thanks to free, open source content management systems, it is possible to deploy and frequently update a sophisticated website at a very reasonable cost.

* *Text messaging and microblogging. (Tools: Twitter)*
The cost of cell phone text messaging has fallen drastically in recent years, allowing Twitter subscribers to receive a constant torrent of text messages at low cost. Since the limitations of cell phone technology restrict such text messages to around 160 characters, messages usually sent via Twitter, known as "tweets," tend to be very short and have a spur-of-the-moment, personal nature. Twitter can

also be used to simply update readers of new content on your blog or podcast.

CONTENT-PROMOTION TOOLS

- *Social networking sites. (Examples: Facebook, MySpace, and Friendster)*

Social networking sites allow users to maintain a personalized home page, or "profile," establish online friendships with others, and share information with one another. It is common practice for organizations, candidates and book authors to create profiles on social networking sites, and to encourage their members, constituents, and fans to connect with those profiles. In fact, Facebook recently launched functionality specifically geared to this practice. Organizations may now create "Pages" and Facebook members may become "fans" of these pages. Online relationships of this sort allow Facebook users to promote a cause to their friends. They also provide organizations with a way to find and communicate with prospective members.

- *Social bookmarking. (Examples: Digg, StumbleUpon, and Del.icio.us)*

On a social bookmarking site, users create accounts and keep track of sites they like. While the primary purpose of these sites is to keep track of one's favorite websites, articles, and other online media, these sites also allow users to establish friendships with one another, like social networking sites. Users may share their accumulated bookmarks with friends, and discover interesting sites their friends have marked. These sites can be also be used by an organization's members to send organizational messages to their friends and colleagues.

- *Media sharing sites. (Examples: YouTube and Flickr)*

These sites allow users to upload photos, video, or other multimedia content, share it with other users, as well as rate and comment on the material. Moreover, users can establish online friendships, and can browse the content their friends have posted or ranked highly. Finally, users can display content from a media sharing site anywhere else on the web, without worrying about the cost of storing and maintaining that content. This allows an organization to communicate a compelling message in a rich format, as well as receive rich media, like videos and photographs, from their members.

- *Political networking sites. (Examples: DFA-Link, Party Builder, and MyBarackObama)*
There are a small number of social networking sites that are specifically designed to support the work of grassroots political organizers. These sites make it easy for activists to gather into local groups, plan and promote events and meetings, send email to one another, share documents, raise money, pressure politicians, gather petition signatures, and do many of the other important tasks required for effective political organizing.

CRAFTING A STRATEGY AND KNOWING WHAT TO EXPECT

You may notice a striking similarity among these tools. All of them feature dynamic, user-generated content. Most have a low start-up cost. Accounts on Blogger, Facebook, Twitter, and other services are free. And almost all of them require only a low-level of technical skill. Still, organizers will want to ensure that people know the basics before assuming that they will use these tools. Therefore, some training may be required.

More than that, we should emphasize that these tools are interactive, helping people learn from one another, share information and analysis, debate and more. These are also tools for political mobilization. Indeed, some are already in use by many organizations large and small, as well as by candidates for public office.

Since this sounds so promising, you may be thinking, "Great, Monday I'll start my blog, Tuesday I'll set up my Facebook account... and by Saturday, my media empire will be complete and the donations will start rolling in..." However, while almost all of these new media tools have a low barrier to entry and facilitate action, creating a successful promotion effort in any one of them requires a significant investment of time spent creating new content and networking with users.

Thus, we recommend starting small. Learn to use one or two tools well, devoting time to consistently adding new content through those tools, and responding to user feedback. It may make sense to have one tool (such as a blog) where you put your primary content and accept feedback from constituents; and a second tool (such as Facebook or StumbleUpon) that you use to reach additional users and promote the primary content. Different tools will work for different organizations, naturally; there's no "one size fits all" solution. To devise a good online communication strategy, you need to start by identifying your core goals, determine who your audience is and how they can be reached, and choose tools that allow you to mobilize your constituents to meet your goals. Along the way, expect to get feedback, and don't expect it all to be constructive and positive. (Or even correctly spelled.) But do listen carefully to what people are saying—and respond. Interactive media provides a learning and skill building environment, and the feedback and advice you get can be invaluable.

In closing, it is simpler than you might think to compose a successful online strategy using these tools—and to contribute to how the Religious Left as a whole uses new media to create progressive change.

THE RELIGIOUS LEFT'S LONG-TERM FUNDING CHALLENGE

⇐

REV. PETER LAARMAN

I will first state the challenge as succinctly as I can, then turn to the broken conversation between progressive religious leaders and (mostly) secular progressive funders, and then offer a menu of capacity-related vehicles that merit sustained funding. What I mean by "capacity" is the institutional and financial infrastructure that undergirds the work of any organization over the long haul. The strength of this infrastructure ultimately determines whether an institution or network of institutions can carry out a mission that is greater than the sum of short-term, albeit worthwhile, projects.

Here then is a core problem for the Religious Left: Much of the funding that is currently available puts at risk the mission, integrity and long-term transformational capacity of worthy and hard-working organizations. I refer to the well-documented reality that while progressive religious social justice groups can sometimes get funding for specific short-term projects relating to the donor's agenda, they are almost never funded to build their long-term organizational capacities. Because most Religious Left groups—and I mean groups that bring a sharp progressive critique of the distribution of wealth and power—are small and under-resourced to begin with, they can fatally weaken their existing capacity by chasing unattainable money or by agreeing to serve a particular funder's agenda in ways that compromise their core mission. Chasing the available money can also confuse and alienate their core individual supporters and boards of directors.

Project-related grants normally support one-or two-year projects and allow a maximum of 15 percent in "overhead" for the support of the group's administrative costs. Secular funders can be particularly vigilant in scrutinizing the overhead portion, because the last thing they want to be doing is supporting "religion" per se. Many leaders of grant-seeking groups I have interviewed believe that the allowable overhead in project grants should move toward the 40 percent level in order to nurture and not retard organizational development.

Before I turn to what I call the broken conversation between secular funders and Religious Left organizations, let me clear away some possible misunderstandings.

1. I am necessarily generalizing in this essay. I do not mean to disparage those secular funders who already see the strategic value of supporting progressive religious organizing and who do, in fact, make capacity-building grants to progressive religious groups.

2. Leaders of religious non-profits who are ineffective fundraisers are often too quick to blame the funders; or worse, to impute an anti-religious bias even when there is zero evidence to support such an imputation.

3. I'm not discussing the funding of faith-based community organizing in this essay. For three decades, secular and religious funders have poured many millions into the organizing efforts of Saul Alinsky's three institutional progeny: the Industrial Areas Foundation, the Gamaliel Foundation, and the PICO National Network. These groups enjoy a relatively strong fund-

ing base, but in my view they are unlikely to become a strong public voice for major social change. They tend to stay under the public policy radar, focusing instead on winning small concrete victories for poor communities—a worthy activity but not a prophetic one.

4. I am also not addressing the funding of traditional denominational structures, seminaries, and parachurch organizations that may have a progressive tilt but that are not primarily focused on politics and public policy. My focus is on funding for what I would call "outsider" organizations, not inside players.

Turning now to the broken conversation:

Many secular funders are unable to distinguish adequately between foam-at-the-mouth Fundamentalism and a reasoned progressive faith. Those who have drunk deeply at the wells of Sam Harris or Christopher Hitchens or Richard Dawkins tend to be contemptuous of all people of faith. To them it's all dangerous hokum.

On the other side of the broken conversation are Religious Left leaders who may be equally mistrustful and may also feel that the importance of their work is so self-evident that there is no need to make a case for long-term funding. Everyone knows of small progressive religious groups that waste time and postage sending poorly-framed proposals to major foundations, only to take the lack of response as evidence of ignorance or bias or both within the grantmaking community.

We can begin to fix the broken conversation by focusing on work being done by the Religious Left that intersects the primary concerns of progressive funders. For example, Religious Left activists recognize and deplore the decay of healthy civic discourse and the measurable decline in civic participation over recent decades. Like progressive funders, Religious Left leaders seek to counter corrosive cynicism while still acknowledging and even highlighting the nasty reality that much of contemporary politics boils down to well-heeled interest groups gaming the system to their own advantage and profit.

Here are some ways by which the Religious Left helps revitalize a democratic politics:

- Progressive religious groups equip people to engage issues in the public square and do so in a respectful and potentially persuasive way—in a way that is antithetical to the shouting of both the Religious Right and also of some parts of the Secular Left.

- Progressive religion is not an "interest group": its "interest" is in achieving a healthy, functioning, society with opportunity for all. In this it differs sharply from the justly-loathed interest groups that show no concern for the commonwealth.

- Progressive religious groups have a deep understanding of the need for separation of church and state woven into their DNA. These groups are uniformly against so-called "faith-based initiatives" because of the way these subsidies to religious groups lead to religious and or gender/sexual discrimination. Because they have religious reasons for opposing such state subsidies and all theocratic currents, they cannot easily be dismissed as "godless secularists" and the spawn of Satan.

- Because progressive religious groups renew people's hopes and replenish their energies even while taking a realistic view of entrenched evil power, they provide a strong antidote to despair and cynicism wit in the common culture.

Another area of important convergence: progressive funders are focused today on complex social issues—survival issues—that cannot be solved in the absence of the kind of deep-level cultural change that the Religious Left seeks to catalyze. Three (among many) such issues are climate change and sustainability, the U.S. military-imperial stance toward the rest of the world, and the corrosive "culture of distraction" represented by proliferating junk media and unchecked consumerism—a culture that fatally undermines the educational system and threatens the health of democracy itself.

- Progressive religion brings to bear a profound critique of the notion that twenty-first century Americans are somehow entitled to lives of unlimited consumption. As Chris Hedges has written, belief in God may not be essential but belief in "original sin" is in fact increasingly essential in order for Americans to start recognizing limits to their consumption and also start recognizing the crucial difference between a truly good life and a life stuffed with goods. More than this, progressive religion contains within it a strong critique of unjust wealth that readily lends itself to a sweeping critique of free market dogma. This critique of market fundamentalism matters strategically at a time when people are finally seeing how so-called free trade has mainly benefited economic elites and entrenched corporate interest while leaving everyone else worse off and contributing greatly to the looming environmental catastrophe.

- Progressive religion is uncompromising in teaching that it is not just particular wars but the entire war system (a system rooted in patriarchy, misogyny, imperial hubris, and bad religion) that now needs to be scrutinized and transformed. In particular, progressive religion supplies a much-needed tonic against the delusional and dangerous idea that the United States enjoys a special divine providence and is thus exempt from having to explain itself or show respect for other peoples and cultures. Progressive religion shatters the myth of America's "original innocence" that has led to so much folly and caused so much grief and suffering over the centuries.

- Progressive religion militates against the culture of distraction by creating intimate spaces in which people can help each other escape both the false consciousness of consumerism and the shrill sloganeering and hucksterism of the corporate media—what Robert Jay Lifton once called "the thought-terminating cliché."

I have sketched the convergence of core interest between secular funders and Religious Left organizers. Funders rightly want to know exactly how good social outcomes can result from this convergence. They want to see some vehicles for turning the Religious Left's righteous passion into righteous performance.

Here is a brief listing of potentially potent vehicles and tools that are mainly missing from the progressive religious armamentarium today—vehicles that, if fully funded, would make that armamentarium much more strategically effective.

- Web-based resources. Growing numbers of progressive faith bloggers and a few decent web sites are out there now, but there is nothing with anything close to the depth, scale, and reach required in this thoroughly wired era. We need something approaching the richness and speed of *The Huffington Post*—something with breaking news, commentary, blogs, humor, and lots of culture criticism.

- Think tanks. Anyone who understands how idea generation and movement building are intimately linked should be asking why progressive religion gets almost no money to develop and articulate ideas, books and articles—unlike such well endowed institutions of the Religious Right as the Action Institute, Institute on Religion and Public Life, Institute on Religion and Democracy, Faith and Reason Institute, Family Research Council, etc.

- Media training. This is closely related to the need to support substantive thinking. The good framing and good ideas will have no traction in changing the culture without cadres of trained, nimble messengers.

- Next-generation leadership development. Right-wing religious groups like Campus Crusade for Christ and the Intervarsity Christian Fellowship take in roughly $1 billion each year to ensure the future vitality of the conservative Christian voice. Moderate-to-progressive spiritual support groups hardly exist on U.S. college campuses any longer. Because of this, students with progressive religious backgrounds sometimes turn their back on religion altogether, while students migrating away from conservative backgrounds have no place to go. Many of both kinds of students would welcome conversations in which faith and its relationship to activism can be explored with sensitivity.

- Regional networking resources. Progressive people of faith need to find and support each other regionally and locally outside of denominational lines and outside of various issue "silos." My own group—Progressive Christians Uniting—has created a working model for how such networks can be nurtured and grown.

- Progressive clergy training and support. Few understand the loneliness of the prophetic preacher/teacher—or the very high burnout and/or termination rate among those who lead from an unabashedly progressive platform. We urgently need a replicable training/support vehicle that can function as a lifeline for these leaders, not just keeping them in the ministry but helping them really flourish and build strong congregations around a core progressive message.

- Citizen participation training. This would include but not be limited to training in voter registration and mobilization and in the mechanics of issue advocacy and electoral politics, thus linking visions of social change to practical tools for making such visions come to life in actual public policy.

I Don't Believe in Atheists

⇐

CHRIS HEDGES

Editor's Note: On May 22, 2007, Chris Hedges and "new atheist" author Sam Harris debated "Religion, Politics and the End of the World," as a fundraiser for the online news site, Truthdig. This is Hedges' opening statement in which the former New York Times war correspondent and Harvard Divinity student, demonstrates that a progressive person of faith who is engaged in politics and public debate does not have to manifest milquetoastery or issue false appeals to common ground in the defense of faith, the principles that flow from it.

Sam Harris has conflated faith with tribalism. His book (*The End of Faith*) is an attack not on faith but on a system of being and believing that is dangerous and incompatible with the open society. He attacks superstition, a belief in magic and the childish notion of an anthropomorphic God that is characteristic of the tribe, of the closed society. He calls this religion. I do not.

What he fails to grasp is not simply the meaning of faith—something I will address later—but the supreme importance of the monotheistic traditions in creating the concept of the individual. This individualism—the belief that we can exist as distinct beings from the tribe, or the crowd, and that we are called on as individuals to make moral decisions that at times defy the clamor of the tribe or the nation—is a gift of the Abrahamic faiths. This sense of individual responsibility is coupled with the constant injunctions in Islam, Judaism and Christianity for a deep altruism. And this laid the foundations for the open society. This individualism is the central doctrine and most important contribution of monotheism. We are enjoined, after all, to love our neighbor, not our tribe. This empowerment of individual conscience is the starting point of the great ethical systems of our civilization. The prophets—and here I would include Jesus—helped institutionalize dissent and criticism. They initiated the separation of powers. They reminded us that culture and society were not the sole prerogative of the powerful, that freedom and indeed the religious life required us to often oppose and defy those in authority. This is a distinctly anti-tribal outlook. Immanuel Kant built his ethics upon this radical individualism. And Kant's injunction to "always recognize that human individuals are ends, and do not use them as mere means" runs in a direct line from the Christian Gospels. Karl Popper rightly pointed out in the first volume of *The Open Society and Its Enemies*, when he writes about this creation of the individual as set against the crowd, that "There is no other thought which has been so powerful in the moral development of man." These religions set free the critical powers of humankind. They broke with the older Greek and Roman traditions that gods and destiny ruled human fate—a belief that when challenged by Socrates saw him condemned to death. They offered up the possibility that human beings, although limited by circumstances and simple human weaknesses, could shape and give direction to society. And most important, individuals could give direction to their own lives.

Human communication directly shapes the quality of a culture. These believers were being asked to embrace an abstract, universal deity. This deity could not be captured in pictures, statues or any concrete, iconographic form. God exists in the word and through the word, an unprecedented conception in the ancient world that required the highest order of abstract thinking. "In the beginning," the Gospel of John reads, "was the Word, and the Word was with God, and the Word was God." This is why the second of the Ten Commandments prohibits Israelites from making concrete images of God. "Iconography thus became blasphemy," Neil Postman writes, "so that a new kind of God could enter a culture."

God is a human concept. God is the name we give to our belief that life has meaning, one that transcends the world's chaos, randomness and cruelty. To argue about whether God exists or does not exist is futile. The question is not whether God exists. The question is whether we concern ourselves with, or are utterly indifferent to, the sanctity and ultimate transcendence of human existence. God is that mysterious force—and you can give it many names as other religions do—which works upon us and through us to seek and achieve truth, beauty and goodness. God is perhaps best understood as our ultimate concern, that in which we should place our highest hopes, confidence and trust. In Exodus God says, by way of identification, "I am that I am." It is probably more accurately translated: "I will be what I will be." God is better understood as verb rather than a noun. God is not an asserted existence but a process accomplishing itself. And God is inescapable. It is the life force that sustains, transforms and defines all existence. The name of God is laden, thanks to our religious institutions and the numerous tyrants, charlatans and demagogues these institutions produced, with so much baggage and imagery that it is hard for us to see the intent behind the concept. All societies and cultures have struggled to give words to describe these forces. It is why Freud avoided writing about the phenomenon of love.

Faith allows us to trust, rather, in human compassion, even in a cruel and morally neutral universe. This is not faith in magic, not faith in church doctrine or church hierarchy, but faith in simple human kindness. It is only by holding on to the sanctity of each individual, each human life, only by placing our faith in the tiny, insignificant acts of compassion and kindness, that we survive as a community and as a human being. And these small acts of kindness are deeply feared and subversive to institutional religious and political authorities. The Russian novelist Vasily Grossman wrote in *Life and Fate*:

"I have seen that it is not man who is impotent in the struggle against evil, but the power of evil that is impotent in the struggle against man. The powerlessness of kindness, of senseless kindness, is the secret of its immortality. It can never be conquered. The more stupid, the more senseless, the more helpless it may seem, the vaster it is. Evil is impotent before it. The prophets, religious teachers, reformers, social and political leaders are impotent before it. This dumb, blind love is man's meaning. Human history is not the battle of good struggling to overcome evil. It is a battle fought by a great evil struggling to crush a small kernel of human kindness. But if what is human in human beings has not been destroyed even now, then evil will never conquer."

It is by the seriousness of our commitments to compassion, indeed our ability to sacrifice for the other, especially for the outcast and the stranger, our commitment to justice—the very core of the message of the prophets and the teachings of Jesus—that we alone can measure the quality of faith. This is the meaning of true faith. As Matthew wrote. "By their fruits shall you know them." Professed faith—what we say we believe—is not faith. It is an expression of loyalty to a community, to our tribe. Faith is what we do. This is real faith. Faith is the sister of justice. And the prophets reminded us that nothing is exempt from criticism. Revelation is continuous. It points beyond itself. And doubt, as well as a request for forgiveness, must be included in every act of faith, for we can never know or understand the will of God.

The problem is not religion but religious orthodoxy. Most moral thinkers—from Socrates to Christ to Francis of Assisi—eschewed the written word because they knew, I suspect, that once

things were written down they became, in the wrong hands, codi-
fied and used not to promote morality but conformity, subservience
and repression. Writing freezes speech. George Steiner calls this
"the decay into writing." Language is turned from a living and fluid
form of moral inquiry to a tool of bondage.

The moment the writers of the Gospels set down the words of
Jesus they began to kill the message. There is no room for prophets
within religious institutions—indeed within any institutions—for
as Paul Tillich knew, all human institutions, including the church,
are inherently demonic. Tribal societies persecute and silence prophets. Open societies tolerate them at their fringes, and our prophets
today come not from the church but from our artists, poets and
writers who follow their inner authority. Samuel Beckett's voice is
one of modernity's most authentically religious. Beckett, like the
author of Ecclesiastes, was a realist. He saw the pathetic, empty
monuments we spend a lifetime building to ourselves. He knew, as
we read in Ecclesiastes, that nothing is certain or permanent, real
or unreal, and that the secret of wisdom is detachment without
withdrawal, that, since death awaits us all, all is vanity, that we must
give up on the childish notion that one is rewarded for virtue or
wisdom. In Ecclesiastes God has put 'olam into man's mind. 'Olam
usually means eternity, but it also means the sense of mystery or
obscurity. We do not know what this mystery means. It teases us,
as Keats wrote, out of thought. And once we recognize it and face
it, simplistic answers no longer work. We are all born lost. Our vain
belief in our own powers, in our reason, blinds us.

Those who silenced Jesus represented all human societies,
not the Romans or the Jews. When Jesus attacks the chief priests,
scribes, lawyers, Pharisees, Sadducees and other "blind guides" he is
attacking forms of oppression as endemic to Christianity, as to all
religions and all ideologies. If civil or religious authority enforces
an iron and self-righteous conformity among members of a community, then faith loses its uncertainty, and the element of risk is

removed from acts of faith. Faith is then transformed into ideology. Those who deform faith into creeds, who use it as a litmus test for institutional fidelity, root religion in a profane rather than a sacred context. They seek, like all who worship idols, to give the world a unity and coherency it does not possess. They ossify the message. And once ossified it can never reach an existential level, can never rise to ethical freedom—to faith. The more vast the gap between professed faith and acts of faith, the more vast our delusions about our own grandeur and importance, the more intolerant, aggressive and dangerous we become.

Faith is not in conflict with reason. Faith does not conflict with scientific truth, unless faith claims to express a scientific truth. Faith can neither be affirmed nor denied by scientific, historical or philosophical truth. Sam confuses the irrational—which he sees as part of faith—with the non-rational. There is a reality that is not a product of rational deduction. It is not accounted for by strict rational discourse. There is a spiritual dimension to human existence and the universe, but this is not irrational—it is non-rational. Faith allows us to transcend what Flaubert said was our "mania for conclusions," a mania he described as "one of humanity's most useless and sterile drives."

Reason allows us to worship at the idol of our intrinsic moral superiority. It is a dangerous form of idolatry, a form of faith, certainly, but one the biblical writers knew led to evil and eventually self-immolation. "We are at war with Islam," Harris writes. "It may not serve our immediate foreign policy objectives for our political leaders to openly acknowledge this fact, but it is unambiguously so. It is not merely that we are at war with an otherwise peaceful religion that has been 'hijacked' by extremists. We are at war with precisely the vision of life that is prescribed to all Muslims in the Koran, and further elaborated in the literature of the hadith, which recounts the sayings and teachings of the Prophet" (P. 110).

He assures us that "the Koran mandates such hatred" (P. 31), that "the problem is with Islam itself" (P. 28). He writes that "Islam, more than any other religion human beings have devised, has all the makings of a thoroughgoing cult of death" (P. 123).

Now after studying 600 hours of Arabic, spending seven years of my life in the Middle East, most of that time as the Middle East bureau chief for *The New York Times*, I do not claim to be a scholar on Islam. But I do know the Koran is emphatic about the rights of other religions to practice their own beliefs and unequivocally condemns attacks on civilians as a violation of Islam. The Koran states that suicide, of any type, is an abomination. More important, the tactic of suicide bombing was pioneered as a weapon of choice by the Tamils, who are chiefly Hindu, in Sri Lanka long before it was adopted by Hezbollah, al-Qaida or Hamas. It is what you do when you do not have artillery or planes or missiles and you want to create maximum terror.

I also know from my time in the Muslim world that the vast majority of the some 1 billion Muslims on this planet—most of whom are not Arab—are moderate, detest the violence done in the name of their religion and look at the Pat Robertsons and Franklin Grahams, who demonize Muslims in the name of Christianity, with the same horror with which we look at Osama bin Laden or Hamas. The Palestinian resistance movement took on a radical Islam coloring in the 1990s only when conditions in Gaza and the West Bank deteriorated and thrust people into profound hopelessness, despair and poverty—conditions similar to those that empowered the Christian right in our own country. Before that the movement was decidedly secular. I know that Muslim societies are shaped far more by national characteristics—an Iraqi has a culture and out-look on life that are quite different from an Indonesian's—just as a French citizen, although a Catholic, is influenced far more by the traits of his culture. Islam has within it tiny, marginal groups that worship death, but nearly all suicide bombers come from one language group within the Muslim world, Arabic, which represents only 20 percent of Muslims. I have seen the bodies—including the bodies of children—left in the wake of a suicide bombing attack in Jerusalem. But I have also seen the frail, thin bodies of boys shot to death for sport by Israeli soldiers in the Gaza Strip. Tell me the moral difference. I fail to see one, especially as a father.

Finally, let us not forget that the worst genocides and slaughters of the last century were perpetrated not by Muslims but Christians. To someone who lived in Sarajevo during the Serbian siege of the city, Sam's demonization of the Muslim world seems odd. It was the Muslim-led government in Bosnia that practiced tolerance. There were some 10,000 Serbs who remained in the city and fought alongside the Bosnia Muslims during the war. The city's Jewish community, dating back to 1492, was also loyal to the government. And the worst atrocities of the war were blessed not by imams but Catholic and Serbian Orthodox priests. Sam's argument that atheists have a higher moral code is as specious as his attacks on Islam. Does he forget Joseph Stalin, Adolf Hitler and Pol Pot? These three alone filled the earth with more corpses in the last century than all of the world's clerics combined.

The danger is not Islam or Christianity or any other religion. It is the human heart—the capacity we all have for evil. All human institutions with a lust for power give their utopian visions divine sanction, whether this comes through the worship of God, destiny, historical inevitability, the master race, a worker's paradise, *fraternite-egalite-liberte* or the second coming of Jesus Christ.

Religion is often a convenient vehicle for this blood lust. Religious institutions often sanctify genocide, but this says more about us, about the nature of human institutions and the darkest human yearnings, than it does about religion. This is the greatest failing of Sam's book. He externalizes evil. And when you externalize evil, all tools, including violence and torture, become legitimate to eradicate an evil that is outside of you. This worldview—one also adopted by the Christian right—is dangerous, for if we fail to acknowledge our own capacity for evil it will grow unchecked and unheeded. It is, in essence, the call to live the unexamined life.

This externalization of evil is what allows Sam to endorse torture. He, of course, deludes himself into believing that it is reason that requires us to waterboard detainees in the physical and moral black holes we have set up to make them disappear. He quotes Alan Dershowitz, not only to reassure us that the Israelis treat Palestinians—400 of whom they have killed in Gaza over the past few months—humanely, but to trot out the absurd notion of a ticking time bomb, the idea that we know a terrorist has planted a large bomb in the center of the city and we must torture him, or in the glib phrase of Harris, we must dust off "a strappado" and expose "this unpleasant fellow to a suasion of bygone times" (P. 193).

I guess this reference to torture is amusing if you have spent your life encased in the protected world of the university. As someone who was captured and held for over a week by the Iraqi Republican Guard during the 1991 Shiite uprising in Basra and then turned over for my final 24 hours to the Iraqi secret police—who my captors openly expected to execute me—I find this glib talk of physical abuse repugnant. Dershowitz and Harris cannot give us a legal or historical precedent where such a case as they describe actually happened. But this is not the point; the point is to endow themselves with the moral right to abuse others in the name of their particular version of goodness. This is done in the name of reason. It is done in the name of a false god, an idol. And this god—if you want it named—is the god of death, or as Freud stated, Thanatos, the death instinct, the impulse that works toward the annihilation of all living things, including ourselves. For once you torture, done in the name of reason, done to make us safe, you unleash sadists and killers. You consign some human beings to moral oblivion. You become no better than those you oppose.

The danger of Sam's simplistic worldview is that it does what fundamentalists do: It creates the illusion of a binary world of us and them, of reason versus irrationality, of the forces of light battling the forces of darkness. And once you set up this world you are permitted to view as justified military intervention, brutal occupation and even torture, anything, in short, that will subdue what is defined as irrational and dangerous. All this is done in the name of reason, in the name of his god, which looks, like all idols, an awful lot like Sam Harris. "Necessity," William Pitt wrote, "is the plea for every infringement of human freedom."

Sam ends his book with a chapter that can best be described as Buddhism light. His spirituality, which apparently includes life after death and telepathy, fuels our narcissistic obsession with our individual unconscious. I am not against solitude or meditation, but I support it only when it feeds the moral life rather than serves as an excuse to avoid moral commitment. The quest for personal fulfillment can become an excuse for the individual to negate his or her responsibilities as a citizen, as a member of a wider community. Sam's religion—for Sam in an odd way tries at the end of his book to create one—is in tune with this narcissism. His idealized version of Buddhism is part of his inability to see that it too has been used to feed the lusts of warriors and killers; it too has been hijacked in the name of radical evil. Buddhist Shinto warrior cults justified and absolved those who carried out the worst atrocities committed by the Japanese in Nanjing. By the end of World War II Buddhist and Shinto priests recruited and indoctrinated kamikaze (divine wind) pilots in the name of another god. It is an old story. It is not the evil of religion, but the inherent capacity for evil of humankind.

The point of religion, authentic religion, is that it is not, in the end, about us. It is about the other, about the stranger lying beaten and robbed on the side of the road, about the poor, the outcasts, the marginalized, the sick, the destitute, about those who are being abused and beaten in cells in Guantanamo and a host of other secret locations, about what we do to gays and lesbians in this country, what we do to the 47 million Americans without health insurance, the illegal immigrants who live among us without rights or protection, their suffering as invisible as the suffering of the mentally ill we have relegated to heating grates or prison cells. It is about them.

We have forgotten who we were meant to be, who we were created to be, because we have forgotten that we find God not in ourselves, finally, but in our care for our neighbor, in the stranger, including those outside the nation and the faith. The religious life is not designed to make you happy, or safe or content; it is not designed to make you whole or complete, to free you from anxieties and fear; it is designed to save you from yourself, to make possible human community, to lead you to understand that the greatest force in life is not power or reason but love. As Reinhold Niebuhr wrote:

> Nothing worth doing is completed in our lifetime,
> Therefore, we are saved by hope.
> Nothing true or beautiful or good makes complete sense in
> any immediate context of history;
> Therefore, we are saved by faith.
> Nothing we do, however virtuous, can be accomplished
> alone.
> Therefore, we are saved by love.
> No virtuous act is quite as virtuous from the standpoint of
> our friend or foe as from our own;
> Therefore, we are saved by the final form of love which is
> forgiveness.

AFTERWORD

⇐

JEFF SHARLET

It's not working.

But it could.

The "it" in those two short sentences—diagnosis and prognosis—is the Religious Left that's at the heart of this book, the movement-that-is-not-(yet)-a-movement. Too many of the recent books about the Religious Left declare easy victory, the triumph of modest faith and mild-mannered reason over vulgar fundamentalism. This one predicts a hard and uncertain fight, against not just a Religious Right more vital and sophisticated than commonly imagined but also the limited imagination of the Religious Left, as currently constituted. The essays gathered here draw on memory—most powerfully that of Martin Luther King, Jr.—and hint at a new vision even as they proceed from the unavoidable conclusion that American religious leftists lack one. This book isn't the vision; that's still to come. Rather, it's something more exciting, more kinetic, more democratic: a collection of clues, leads, lessons learned, successful experiments, potential tactics, glimmers of—there's no other word for it—that much-abused, worn-thin, still-sparking notion, "hope."

But hope, the cultural critic Cornel West reminds us, isn't a symptom of imminent victory, it's what you have when reason alone leads you to despair. As writers including Frederick Clarkson, "Pastor Dan" Schultz, and the Reverend Osagyefo Sekou make clear in these pages, the weak alliance of amiable evangelicals, well-intentioned mainline Protestants, old school social justice Catholics, and Michael Lerner that's currently heralded by mainstream media as a resurgent Religious Left is neither left nor surging. Rather, it's a centrist coalition of the willing that's reporting for duty—not to the task of prophetically challenging power but to a Democratic Party bent on peeling off undecided voters. The religious centrists call this initiative "faith outreach," an ironic label for a process that is neither faithful—to the core value of both democracy and most of the believers involved, which is that everybody counts—nor particularly reaching anyone.

As the Reverend Barry Lynn reminds us, the Religious Right remains strong, if in flux. Religious conservatism's new interest in global warming and AIDS aren't signs of a chastened movement but of an emboldened one, a movement broadening its concerns and its influence as it discards the angry old men whose fury propelled it into the mainstream. The Religious Right isn't dead; it's been institutionalized.

And the lukewarm Democratic Party appendage that passes for a Religious Left isn't so much offering a different vision than the Religious Right as a different version. It's an ostensibly "kinder, gentler way to do politics," as Pastor Dan notes, that in truth is simultaneously cynical and naïve: a crass attempt by Democratic Party hacks to make of religious leftists a loyal and unquestioning base; and a sincere effort by self-declared centrists to "transcend politics," as if the rough and tumble of democracy, the sharp elbows of real debate, and the painful truths of prophecy were unpleasant distractions, best euphemized and then euthanized, sacrificed for the sake of "common ground."

But life, Darwin reminds us, is not a value, it's a fact, and one defined not by harmony but by struggle. The good news is that that is the good news: the rowdy, pluralist approach to politics embraced by religious leftists is the fundamental faith of America. Not perfect harmony; glorious cacophony. "The noise of democracy," according to President James Buchanan, who was a failure in nearly every respect but for the high regard in which he held the American sacrament of *arguing*.

Brothers and sisters: Let us argue. It's what we do best. "The genius of the Religious Left," Pastor Dan proposes, "has never been in organizational heft or the ability to mobilize campaign contributions or stick to talking points pumped out of the blast-faxes of suburban Virginia. Progressive faith has been generative instead in its eternal, persistent, damnably disruptive questioning of the seemingly self-evident way things must be." That's *Dispatches from the Religious Left*. It's not ameliorative; it's damnably disruptive. Just because we don't believe in "culture war" doesn't mean we're all on the same side.

Several years ago, my friend Peter Manseau and I wrote a book called *Killing the Buddha: A Heretic's Bible*, for which we spent close to a year wandering what we came to term the "margins of faith" in America, interviewing not (self) important religious leaders but just living and occasionally praying with ordinary believers: a divinely inspired tornado chaser in Oklahoma, a pagan "crone" retired from the Air Force in Kansas, a "cowboy preacher" in rural Texas. The cowboy preacher, a rancher named George McVeigh who led a little church in a manger, literally, happened to be of a fundamentalist persuasion. Apart from his conviction that cattle enjoyed a standing before Christ equal to that of humans, his theology matched up neatly with that of his better-known Texas colleague in ministry, John Hagee. And yet, he welcomed us into his church. He prayed for us. Hell, he even prayed for our book, even though he had no illusions about its contents or its authors.

That's not quite right; he mistook us for a gay couple. Pastor

George didn't much like the idea of homosexuality, but he liked us well enough. And it wasn't one of those "hate the sin, love the sinner" bait-and-switch kind of deals, either. It was a matter of honest disagreement: about who you're allowed to have sex with, what happens when you die, and whether cows go to heaven. George made converts of us on that last point, but there was no reconciliation to be had otherwise. And still, George prayed for us. He didn't transcend anything. He stood his ground and respected us for standing ours.

That's what *this* book does. The writers and activists gathered here span the spectrum from liberal to left, from electorally-inclined to the theologically revolutionary. But none of them are willing to give an inch on that core value of both democracy and American faith: the conviction that *everybody*—soccer moms and sex workers, cowboy preachers and radical faeries—counts. The new religious centrists too often forget that fact. What we learn from this collection is that for the Religious Left to merit capitalization, for it to be a real movement, it's going to need to bring the liberals and leftists and all the wild-eyed ones together.

The movement that can do that doesn't exist. But it could. The pieces are all around us. Frederick Clarkson reminds us that many of the foundations have already been laid—and built upon by organizers who recognized that democracy is not something that just happens on its own but something you make fresh every day. In Fred's home state of Massachusetts, groups like Neighbor-to-Neighbor and Boston Vote are *making* democracy happen. Jean Hardisty and Deepak Bhargava raid the Religious Right to reclaim the strategies they adopted from the activist left—not "message discipline" but ideological diversity and a recognition that electoral politics are nothing more than a means, never an end. And numerous writers report on the small victories that, gathered together here, begin to reveal a pattern, the possibility of greater things. "Hope is specific, not abstract," Marshall Ganz reminds us. "What's the vision? When

God inspires the Israelites in Exodus, he doesn't offer a vague hope of 'better days,' but describes a land 'flowing with milk and honey' and what must be done to get there. A vision of hope can unfold a chapter at a time."

So here's another chapter, but the vision is far from complete. It's not even coherent, yet. This book doesn't give us the vision. This "chapter" isn't a manifesto. It's a manual for writing one. Or two, or a thousand. If you've read this far, you probably have a better idea of what it might look like than any one of the contributors on his or her own. Which means, of course, that next chapter is yours. The Religious Left is waiting.

CONTRIBUTORS

Frederick Clarkson is an independent writer, editor, and lecturer who has written about politics and religion for twenty-five years. He is the author of *Eternal Hostility: The Struggle Between Theocracy and Democracy* (Common Courage Press, 1997); co-author of *Challenging the Christian Right: The Activist's Handbook*, (Institute for First Amendment Studies 1992; Ms. Foundation edition, 1994); and editor of *A Moment to Decide: The Crisis in Mainstream Presbyterianism* (Institute for Democracy Studies, 2000). His articles have appeared in numerous magazines and newspapers including *Salon.com*, *Mother Jones*, *Ms.*, *Church & State*, *Conscience*, *Sojourners*, and *The Christian Science Monitor*, and his-op-eds have been nationally syndicated by Knight Ridder. He is the co-founder of the group blog *Talk to Action* (www.talk2action.org) and was a founder of Progressive Democrats of Massachusetts. He is a member of the editorial board of *The Public Eye* magazine. He has appeared on *The CBS Evening News*, ABC's *20/20*, NPR's *All Things Considered*, *Fresh Air*, *Talk of the Nation*, *Democracy Now*, and many other domestic and international radio and television programs.

Rev. Dr. Joan Brown Campbell is the Director of the Department of Religion at the Chautauqua Institution, a 134-year old center for art, education, religion and recreation. As the Director of Religion, she serves as spiritual leader and chaplain for the Institution. Dr. Campbell, formerly General Secretary of the National Council of Churches USA, and Director of the US Office of the World Council of Churches, is an ordained minister with standing in the American Baptist Church and the Christian Church Disciples of Christ.

Jeff Sharlet, an associate research scholar at New York University's Center for Religion and Media, is the author of a bestselling history of elite Christian conservatism, *The Family: The Secret Fundamentalism at the Heart of American Power*, (Harper Collins, 2008), and co-author, with Peter Manseau, of *Killing the Buddha: A Heretic's Bible* (Free Press), named by *Publishers Weekly* one of the ten best religion titles of 2004. Sharlet is a contributing editor for *Harper's* and *Rolling Stone*, the creator of *TheRevealer.org*, a review of religion and media, and co-founder of *KillingTheBuddha.com*, an online literary magazine about religion and culture. His work has also appeared in *Mother Jones, Nation, New Republic, New Statesman, Washington Post, Dallas Morning News, Jewish Forward, Religion Dispatches*, and *Pakn Treger*, the world's only English-language magazine of Yiddish culture. Ann Coulter has dubbed Sharlet one of the "stupidest" journalists in America.

Chip Berlet is senior analyst at Political Research Associates in the Boston area. For over 25 years he has written about civil liberties, social justice, right-wing groups, prejudice, systems of oppression, and scapegoating. Berlet is co–author of *Right-Wing Populism in America: Too Close for Comfort* (Guilford, 2000) and editor of *Eyes Right! Challenging the Right Wing Backlash* (South End Press, 1995), both of which received a Gustavus Myers Center Award for outstanding scholarship on human rights and bigotry in North America. Berlet's byline has appeared in publications ranging from the *New York Times* and *Boston Globe* to the *Progressive* and *Amnesty Now*. He has appeared on *Nightline, The Today Show*, NPR's *All Things Considered, Democracy Now*, and many other radio and television programs.

Frank L. Cocozzelli is a private practice attorney who lives with his family in New York City. He is a director of the Institute for Progressive Christianity, on behalf of which he co-authored with Eve Herold the *White Paper, An Unholy Alliance: How Neoconservatives and the Religious Right Have Joined Forces to Fight Stem Cell*

Research. He is also the author of a 2008 study published in *The Public Eye* magazine, "How Roman Catholic Neocons Peddle Natural Law into Debates about Life and Death." He writes a weekly column on neoconservatives and the Catholic Right on the *Talk to Action* website, and is currently working on a book on contemporary liberalism.

Kety Esquivel has over ten years of experience in the domestic and international non-profit, private and political sectors. She directed the Latino outreach for the Clark Presidential Campaign and served as the Communications Director for Latinos for America. She spent three years coaching executives on issues of human capital and diversity with Kodak's U.S., Canada and Latin American regional operations. She graduated from Cornell University where she served as the elected student representative on the Board of Trustees. She is pursuing graduate studies in public policy and is co-author and co-editor of the forthcoming books, *Crashing la Pachanga: The Dawn of a New Latino/a Movement,* and *The Coming of Age: Passing the torch of the Latino Movement.* She founded Cross-Left.org and is the Board Chair of the Institute for Progressive Christianity. She serves on the boards of the New Leaders Council; the Backbone Campaign; and is a founder of *The Sanctuary.*

Dr. Marshall Ganz, the son of a Rabbi and teacher, grew up in Bakersfield, California, but left Harvard College in 1964 before completing his studies to volunteer in the Civil Rights Movement in Mississippi, where he discovered a vocation for organizing. In the fall of 1965, he joined Cesar Chavez and the United Farm Workers. During his sixteen years with the UFW, he learned union, community, issue and political organizing, became Organizing Director, and served on the national executive board for eight years. He has since designed organizing programs with union, electoral, issue, and community groups; formed an institute to recruit, train and develop organizers; researched causes of decline in civic engagement, and worked with mayoral, Congressional, Senate, and Presidential campaigns. In 1991 he returned to Harvard, completed his undergraduate work, and went on to earn an MPA from the Kennedy School of Government, and a Ph.D. in sociology. He currently serves as a Lecturer in Public Policy at the Kennedy School. He has published in the *American Prospect, American Journal of Sociology, American Political Science Review, Social Science History*, and elsewhere. His first book, co-authored with Theda Skocpol and Ariane Liazos, *What a Mighty Power We Can Be: African American Fraternal Groups and the Struggle for Racial Equality*, was published in 2006. A new book, *Why David Sometimes Wins: leadership, organization and strategy in the unionization of California agriculture*, is forthcoming from Oxford.

Rev. Debra W. Haffner is co-founder and director of the Religious Institute on Sexual Morality, Justice, and Healing in Westport, Connecticut, a national, multifaith advocacy organization dedicated to sexual health, education and justice in faith communities and society. She is a sexologist, ordained Unitarian Universalist minister and author of six books and numerous congregational resources on parenting, sexuality and spirituality. She is the former president and CEO of SIECUS, the Sexuality Information and Education Council of the U.S.

Dr. Jean Hardisty is the Founder and President Emerita of Political Research Associates (PRA), a Boston-based research center that analyzes right wing, authoritarian, and anti-democratic trends and publishes educational materials for the general public. A political scientist with a Ph.D. from Northwestern University, she left academia after eight years of teaching and researching conservative political thought to establish PRA in response to the emergence of the New Right in 1981. After twenty-three years, she retired from PRA in 2004 and is now a Senior Scholar at the Wellesley Centers for Research on Women at Wellesley College. Dr. Hardisty is a widely published author and has been an activist for social justice issues, especially women's rights and civil rights, for over thirty years. She currently serves on the Board of Directors of the Highlander Research and Education Center and the Women's Community Cancer Project. Her book, *Mobilizing Resentment: Conservative Resurgence from the John Birch Society to the Promise Keepers*, was published by Beacon Press in October 1999 and is now available in paperback. More information can be found at www.jeanhardisty.com

Christopher L. Hedges is a journalist and author, specializing in American and Middle Eastern politics and society. He is currently a senior fellow at The Nation Institute in New York City and a Lecturer in the Council of the Humanities and the Anschutz Distinguished Fellow at Princeton University. He has a B.A. in English Literature from Colgate University and a Master of Divinity from Harvard Divinity School. He spent nearly two decades as a foreign correspondent reporting from more than fifty countries working for *The Christian Science Monitor*, *National Public Radio*, *Dallas Morning News* and *New York Times,* where he spent fifteen years. Hedges was part of the *New York Times* team that won the 2002 Pulitzer Prize for the paper's coverage of global terrorism. He received the 2002 Amnesty International Global Award for Human Rights Journalism. His books include: *War Is a Force That Gives Us Meaning,* (2002) *What Every Person Should Know About War* (2003), *Losing Moses on the Freeway* (2005), *American Fascists* (2007) and *I Don't Believe in Atheists* (2008).

Dr. Peter M. J. Hess serves as Faith Project Director with the National Center for Science Education in Oakland, California. In this capacity he facilitates dialogue between religious and scientific communities in matters of evolutionary biology. Educated at Oxford University and the Graduate Theological Union (Berkeley, CA), he is currently on the faculty of the Graduate Liberal Studies Program at Saint Mary's College (Moraga, California). A fellow of the International Society for Science and Religion, he is co-author of *Catholicism and Science* (Greenwood, 2008), and he is working on a book on the religious and ethical implications of the approaching end of affordable oil.

Rev. Peter Laarman has led Progressive Christians Uniting (PCU) as its executive director since April 2004. His primary focus in Southern California has been building the network's infrastructure while developing new campus outreach and eco-justice projects. He is also part of an ongoing national conversation on the capacity issues facing progressive religious organizations. Before taking his post with PCU, Peter served for ten years as the senior minister of New York's Judson Memorial Church. In 2006 Beacon Press published a book of 14 essays he collected and edited under the rubric, *Getting On Message: Challenging the Christian Right from the Heart of the Gospel.*

Rev. Barry W. Lynn is executive director of Americans United for Separation of Church and State. An attorney as well as an ordained Christian minister, Lynn has been involved in protecting civil and religious liberties all of his professional life. Prior to assuming leadership of Americans United, Lynn worked for the American Civil Liberties Union and the national office of the United Church of Christ. An accomplished public speaker and frequent news media guest, Lynn is the author of *Piety & Politics: The Right-Wing Assault on Religious Freedom* (Harmony, 2006) and coauthor of *First Freedom First: A Citizen's Guide to Protecting Religious Liberty and the Separation of Church and State* (Beacon, 2008).

Leo Maley has worked as a union and political organizer, university lecturer, and think tank researcher. He has been a columnist for the *Amherst Bulletin* as well as a cohost of public affairs programs on Amherst community access TV and on WMUA-FM. His articles syndicated by History News Service have appeared in major newspapers around the country. He is one of the founders of Progressive Democrats of Massachusetts; is a member of the board of Casino Free Massachusetts; and currently chairs the Amherst Democratic Town Committee. He is a graduate of Wesley Theological Seminary in Washington, DC.

Shelby Meyerhoff and Shai Sachs are co-owners of Welcoming Websites, a small business that develops websites for liberal religious congregations and nonprofits.

Ms. Meyerhoff blogs at LookingForFaith.org, where she addresses spirituality and religion from a Unitarian Universalist perspective. She also works at the Unitarian Universalist Association as public witness specialist, and has contributed to the magazine *UU World*. She is a graduate of Harvard Divinity School and Harvard College.

Mr. Sachs blogs at MyDD.com and PlantingLiberally.org, where he discusses strategies for building the progressive movement and liberal entrepreneurship. He has worked as a professional web developer for a wide variety of non-profits since 2003. Mr. Sachs served as the leader of Cambridge Drinking Liberally since 2004, and as the leader of Democracy for America—Cambridge from 2004-2006. He is a graduate of the University of Illinois at Urbana-Champaign and Harvard College.

Timothy Palmer is director of research and communications for the Religious Institute on Sexual Morality, Justice, and Healing in Westport, Connecticut, a national, multifaith advocacy organization dedicated to sexual health, education and justice in faith communities and society. A graduate of Union Theological Seminary in New York, he is a former corporate speechwriter and longtime advocate for lesbian, gay, bisexual and transgender equality.

Anastasia Pantsios is a Cleveland-based writer and photographer who has covered pop music, the arts and politics. Her photos have appeared in such magazines as *Spin*, *Rolling Stone*, the *Village Voice*, the *New York Times*, on record covers and in numerous books. She was a contributing editor to the *Billboard Encyclopedia of Record Producers* (1999). She was associate editor of the alternative newsweekly *Cleveland Free Times*, from September, 2003-July, 2008, where she covered subjects ranging from the Religious Right in Ohio to election reform to the local music scene. She has a master's degree in technical theater and scene design from Case Western Reserve University and is member of Trinity Episcopal Cathedral in downtown Cleveland.

Rev. Dr. Katherine Hancock Ragsdale is the President of Political Research Associates, a progressive think tank based in Somerville, Massachusetts, as well as an Episcopal priest and Vicar of Saint David's Church in Pepperell, Massachusetts. Ragsdale currently serves on the boards of NARAL Pro-Choice America and The White House Project. She speaks widely on issues of Reproductive Justice, LGBTQ equity, and public policy affecting women.

Rev. Daniel Schultz is a United Church of Christ pastor in rural Wisconsin and leader of the online community *Street Prophets*. A graduate of the University of Wisconsin-Madison and Candler School of Theology at Emory University, Reverend Schultz has been an online activist, a local columnist, contributor to many blogs, and originator of the annual Netroots Nation conference, where he conducts an interfaith worship service.

Rev. Osagyefo Uhuru Sekou is the Associate Minister for Social

Justice, Missions, and Community Action at Middle Collegiate Church in the East Village of New York City. A Professor of Preaching at the Seminary Consortium of Urban Pastoral Education, he authored the critically acclaimed *urbansouls* (Urban Press, 2001) and the forthcoming gods, *Gays, and Guns: Religion and the Future of Democracy* (Ig, 2009). Reverend Sekou is an Associate Fellow in Religion and Justice at the Institute for Policy Studies and Freeman Fellow for Interfaith Peace Organizing with the historic Fellowship of Reconciliation. He has studied continental philosophy at the New School and systematic theology at Union Theological Seminary.

Rev. Dr. Carlton W. Veazey is President and CEO of the Religious Coalition for Reproductive Choice (RCRC), the national coalition of religious groups from 15 denominations and faith traditions, and a minister of the National Baptist Convention U.S.A. Growing up in the segregated South, he witnessed the suffering of women who lacked options and opportunity. After a long and distinguished career in church ministry and public service, he joined RCRC in 1996 to continue his ministry for justice and dignity for women and families. During his 11-year tenure as President, RCRC has experienced unprecedented growth at the grassroots and nationally. Reverend Veazey founded the Coalition's celebrated National Black Church Initiative, which is breaking the silence about sexuality in African American churches, and it's South Africa Initiative, which provides HIV/AIDS prevention education in churches and community settings. Nationally, the Coalition has become an increasingly influential voice for reproductive rights and a leader in bringing cultural diversity to the pro-choice movement. Reverend Veazey was chairman of the prestigious Theological Commission of the National Baptist Convention U.S.A. (1989-1992), an organization of more than 7 million members. He is currently pastor of Fellowship Baptist Church in Washington, DC. Reverend Veazey is a graduate of the University of Arkansas at Pine Bluff and Howard University School of Divinity.

ACKNOWLEDGEMENTS

Every book is in many ways a communal project of friends, family and colleagues—and this book is no exception. Thanks and acknowledgements are due to many, and undoubtedly I will miss someone or several someones who deserve recognition. So first to them, my sincere apologies as well as my gratitude.

Thanks to Robert Lasner and Elizabeth Clementson for conceiving of this project and asking me to do it.

Thanks to the contributors whose remarkable words, ideas and vision make this book sing.

Thanks to Steve Swecker, Andrew Weaver, Osagyefo Sekou, Abby Scher, Chip Berlet, and Jonathan Hutson for advice and encouragement at critical junctures; and to Rob Boston, Jackie Witherspoon, Nakisha Eartha, and Marjorie Signer for making things happen.

Thanks to The Wilbraham Public Library where I did much of the work on this book -- and to its wonderful staff and volunteers for proving every day the importance and vitality of public libraries in our community, our culture, and our democracy.

Thanks to Sidney Mills for her friendship, generosity and technical wizardry; and to Frank Cocozzelli for helping me through some rocks and hard places.

Thanks to the late Neta Waracks who meant so much in my life and lives on in much that I do; and to Valeria Thompson for being her friend and mine and an advocate when it mattered.

Thanks to my parents, Frederick and Jean Clarkson for their love and support through it all.

And my deepest gratitude to Kathryn Cornell for everything, always and for keeping hope alive.